glass moon

A REFLECTION OF EVERY WOMAN'S COURAGEOUS BATTLE WITH AGING

MICHELLE PLAYER

Michelle Player

For my daughters, Sawyer & Amelia.

May you age fearlessly.

Table of Contents

Introduction

*"Do Not Regret Growing Older.
It is a privilege denied to many".*
~ Unknown

For me, getting old is scary as hell. As a former choreographer and dance instructor, my identity and ego are strongly attached to the more "youthful" me. Feeling adequate in a competitive world that reduces my worth, the older I get, is not an easy endeavor. As a healthy 51-year-old, I want to physically move as I always have. I want to feel sensual. I want to look in the mirror and accept or even appreciate the numerous changes to my body, skin, and hair. I want to be viewed as a strong and capable woman. Yet, my aging body and mind continues to test my tolerance and grit.

My story is not unusual. Like many women, I have spent a great deal of time and energy unraveling the secrets of youth. The trouble, I've discovered, is that we've all been bamboozled! There is no fountain of youth.

In the following chapters, I reveal my personal story of aging. My words are real and honest in an attempt to bring about an "Aging Enlightenment." This book is not meant to provide all the answers to aging or cite comprehensive research, nor is it meant to be a literary work of art. Instead, I write as a humbled woman feeling extraordinary angst about growing old.

Like a glass window, I will allow an audience to look into the life of a reluctant aging woman and perhaps capture reflections of oneself experiencing similar challenges. Like the untroubled moon putting the day to rest, I hope to parallel the aging process as a peaceful and enlightening conclusion to our inevitable journey. This is my story; this is my Glass Moon.

Part One – My Story

For the devout optimist – you may find that my first three chapters portray aging in a harsh and negative way and wonder why I would share such personal information so candidly. I have no doubt that every reader can relate to some, if not many, of my experiences, but I admit that my language may strike sharply. My intent is to reveal my fear and reluctance to grow old. My journey started with the realization that I did not like what Time was doing to my mind, body, and spirit. I hope you can trust my approach and appreciate the honesty and humor in my critical language.

Chapter 1

My Shelves of Youth Juice

There was a time when I would look at my grandparents' – and now parents' – daily collection of medications and think, "Holy Shit! Takes a lot to keep an old person ticking!" Ironically, I was recently looking at my vanity shelves (four tiers high) and noticing all of the product I use on a daily basis and I thought, "Holy Shit! Takes a lot to keep an aging woman young!"

I am now over a half-century old. That's right… 51 and absolutely dreading the climb. I never imagined myself at this age because I was forever young. Truth is, I don't feel 51. My ego keeps telling me that I am still that attractive, high cheek boned, full head of hair, firm breasted woman who would call the attention of any man passing by. Yet my eyes keep catching glimpses of my naked self, preparing for the shower, and I wonder, "What in the hell happened?"

I recently had to purchase a magnifying mirror in order to properly apply my make-up and pluck all those thick black hairs blasting out of my chin. This purchase seemed helpful at first because my eye sight is definitely waning. However, I find myself discouraged by the reality of what is happening to my face. Like the butter dish left out over a hot summer night, my face is melting. I am not kidding. If I tilt my head sideways, my cheeks fall into my nose range; proof of my dissolving collagen. I also find my face to be a bit morphed in the mornings, with deep indents from a wild sleep pattern. It takes some time for my face to regain its shape. Additionally, the close-up mirror alerts me to the fact that perhaps foundation and eye shadow must go; otherwise it just cakes itself into my wrinkles and expanding pours and makes me look like a dried up show girl. I also realize that the most important product on my shelf, sunscreen, was practically unheard of during my glory years of tanning beds and baby oil.

Although I am generally skeptical of any miracle, I have found myself fully participating in the chase and race for the best products on the market to combat aging. I research, purchase, try, and try again to find the miracle that will give me back ten years and make all my girlfriends envious. I could have taken a nice vacation for what I have spent on anti-wrinkle creams alone in just the last three years. In fact, once when being fingerprinted for a job, I was sent to the FBI lab where my prints could be better detected because they are not readable on the standard print test. No one has an explanation for this. But I do. I theorize that all of these anti-wrinkle creams have made me one of the best candidates for an undetected thief, for I have anti-wrinkled my fingerprints away!

The more invasive procedures to rid my wrinkles, like Botox and fillers, not only scare me a little bit, but are out of my budget. Spending a couple of hundred dollars every few months on ridding my brow frown is not practical. Of course, I've tried these procedures a

4

handful of times, but when no one notices the results, I'm regretful of my vanity.

Along with anti-wrinkle remedies, I desperately try to lengthen, strengthen, and thicken my hair. Back combing went out of style quite some time ago so the alternative is root boosters and fake hair clips. I was never brave enough to get sew-in hair extensions because the maintenance seemed too daunting. So, I resort to hair and nail vitamins, women's Rogaine, collagen peptides, thickening shampoo, red light head helmets, and whatever else will enhance my thinning locks.

The hair on my head seems to find a new home on other parts of my body though, forcing me to add special scissors, tweezers, and anti-hair creams to my shelves. My chin and nostrils are hot spots for healthy hair. My areolas bud random long hairs that are a hurtful bitch to pluck. My crotch has a permanent shadow of dark skin from frequent shaving, giving me yet another reason to avoid being seen in a bathing suit. I attempted laser hair removal for the bikini area but that remedy only lasted about a year.

Make room for mouth products. My winning smile has been invaded by stains from years of drinking coffee, tea, wine, and Diet Coke. And if that isn't sad enough, my teeth are returning to their comfortable, crooked habitat, even after ridiculously expensive braces in adulthood. Receding gum lines have also become an issue, forcing me to pay careful attention to brushing. So, no more brushing while on the can or straightening up the bathroom. Doesn't matter though, can't really multi-task anymore (a different aging discussion).

Ibuprofen and heated muscle creams have a special spot on my shelf; easy to reach (even in the dark). My 40's gifted me with arduous recoveries from workouts along with arthritis. Sometimes I suck down a handful of pain relievers before the onset of pain just to get ahead of the days' expected aches. I find that it's more acceptable to obsess on my aches and pains than when I was younger – so I do.

I must make mention of the hidden spot on my shelf that is home to the creams and salves to aid in various problems with my aging ass and vagina. Hemorrhoids, constipation, Urinary Tract infections, yeast infections, and urinary retention are no simple matter. I have to take several 'before and after' measures when having sex in order to avoid getting a UTI or yeast infection. My southern hemisphere has been the recipient of all sorts of product.

The most dramatic change in my looks would have to be my shape. I was always considered "tiny" and "petite", words I haven't heard to describe me in five years. Somehow, my ass has wandered to the front of my body. What was once a taut booty in back, an inherited trait I am so proud of, has now flattened and given rise to my new bum in front! Seriously, my gut, when naked, looks a lot like an ass; creases and all! The front bum is accentuated by my twin sausage links that spill over my panties whenever I sit down. Hence, the reason I no longer wear underwear. Otherwise known as "muffin top" or "love handles" (names that I find too endearing) have contributed to my insecurity about wearing tight clothing.

My dancer legs, once muscular and tone, have also united with invasive fat cells. If I flex hard enough, I can pull the skin tighter, reducing the look of elephant knees. Yet when not flexed, well… you get the picture.

Strangely, fat has planted itself in the most unexpected places. To clarify, I am not referring to the attractive, curvy, taut, voluptuous meat that many women possess, but the wiggly, dangly, droopy fat that comes with age and loss of muscle mass as well as collagen. I've always had a scrawny upper torso and arms. But now, I am alarmed at the sight of my back fat and skin slurping over the elastic of my bra. I won't be going without a brassiere, however, because aged boobs like to rest below the deck. Throwing me off too, are the arm ornaments that swing when I waive with a raised arm or with any minor movement. And for Hell's sake, when in a push up position (on my knees, of course) I try not to look down at my crepe paper breasts and tummy. That sight can ruin a workout.

Youthful products to combat fat are much harder to find, at least successful ones. Disguising wrinkles or yellow teeth is one thing, but hiding fat and loss of collagen is another. Skin tighteners, tanning lotions, girdles, and spankies are just some of the remedies I have tried. My style, or wardrobe rather, has changed dramatically in order to hide my aging body. Boho dresses and oversized rompers occupy the majority of my closet. Diets and diet pills were a bust; never sustainable. Daily exercise and healthy eating habits are a no brainer to body maintenance, but the work seems to get harder and the results seem to become less noticeable.

Many women, myself included, work hard at keeping our youthful remedies a top secret. We want everyone to think that "I woke up looking this good." We certainly don't want anyone to think that we are vain or shallow enough to invest in products or procedures to make us look younger and more attractive. Yet as women, we are fully aware that looking a specific way in our society will play a significant role in our self-esteem and overall success. Therefore, it is forgivable when we discover a product that actually makes a small improvement to our appearance, that we tightly closet the information from all other female competitors. There is no doubt that our desire to be top of the beauty chain is expensive, exhausting, and strange.

Chasing that fountain of youth became my focus. I thought that by turning back the clock, I could regain my dynamic years of industrious living. I confused myself into thinking that looking young would bring me social approval; for my youthful years had done just that. Yet, all the aging products changed very little for me. I am still growing older and my body is purposefully revealing this process. Like most women, I am in the fight of a lifetime to stay young and valued.

Chapter 2

Women are Warriors

The astounding ability women possess to give birth is both a gift and a nightmare. Seriously, what our bodies go through to bring a life into this world is nothing short of miraculous. Whether you've given birth or not, it's worth recognizing that the female body is of extraordinary design. Moreover, the emotional strength women inherently possess in order to reproduce is remarkable.

I got knocked up at age 28. Ok... I was married and trying for a child. At 110 pounds on the onset of pregnancy, my body experienced a 53-pound weight gain in 9 months – astounding! At the time, this did not bother me much for I was enjoying the attention that pregnant women often receive. Basic manners were extended as people gave up seats, held doors, and carried bags for the waddling, stretched, and swollen woman I was. The attention was welcomed. I also found the tremendous amount of movement going on inside of my body to be entertaining and magical. Somehow, I managed to dodge morning sickness.

The thrills and giggles of pregnancy ended abruptly when my water broke on a record hot day in July of 1998.

As I lay on my couch, in front of the window with the only air conditioning unit in the house, I noticed that my panties were damp. Was it butt sweat? Perhaps pee? I woke my husband, panties in hand, and asked him to "give them a whiff." The good sport he is, he sniffed my panties and admitted, "I don't smell anything." As we debated all the possible liquids in my panties, we decided to call the hospital and see if... I don't know, to see if they could smell anything?

After the phone call, I stood up and a faucet turned on between my legs. We knew the source of liquid must be my water breaking. For the next 20 minutes, I witnessed my husband spin, twirl, question, and fumble as he tried to pull his shit together. He wanted my opinion as to what hat he should wear to the hospital. He took time to carefully pick out music on CD's that he would like to listen to. He made me a diaper out of a garbage bag to protect the car seats, which I refused to wear. He actually asked me if I would like *him* to drive us to the hospital. "Yes", was the answer.

Terrified to have my crotch painfully ripped open, upon arrival, I instantly asked for an epidural, but not before asking for the infamous enema. My biggest concern about giving birth, I kid you not, was that I would slip a turd out on the birthing table in front of my audience. My nerves led me to repeatedly review, in my head, everything I had eaten in the last 24 hours. I spent a long time on the toilet to ensure I was emptied prior to the big show.

Just before pushing, I inquired with the doctor about how I should push. I thought my question was a reasonable one, considering that I was numb from the waist down, but my doctor was very confused. He basically told me to bare down and push like I was going to the bathroom. Oh my God! No wonder I felt anxious about slipping a turd out onto the table. I then inquired with the doctor, "Do I push with ALL my might?" My husband laughed out loud and I gritted my teeth and pushed.

My baby girl weighed 30 pounds – so it seemed. Actually, she was a healthy 8 pounds, 6 ounces, but had an enormous head. After 45 minutes of pushing, with all my might, I finally managed to free the worlds' biggest noggin. Unfortunately, her entrance marks the loss of my vagina. I will not mince words here; my right Labia Majora actually ripped off and fell to the hospital floor along with way too much blood. Code Red.

Ten days later, after swelling subsided, I discovered while bathing and gently washing my vagina with over 100 stitches, that I was missing parts. Alarmed, I grabbed a hand mirror and discovered that I could basically see inside of me! One entire side of my vagina was missing!

This horrific incident was the beginning of a long physical and emotional healing process. I endured many infections as well as surgeries due to the amount of damage to my vagina and rectum. The rectum was sewn back together, but done so in a funky way. I was left with a ball of skin that protruded from my anus (much like a permanent hemorrhoid) that would bleed with most bowel movements. My female anatomy on the inside did not fare well either. Nerve endings were damaged, making tampons and intercourse incredibly painful. My bladder had prolapsed causing me to pee my pants at the whisper of a breeze.

It would be years later that I am able to have the necessary reconstructive surgery. Skin from my anus was used to create a Labia Majora. This procedure was

11

certainly not for correcting the looks of my vagina, for I had no intention of posing nude. But I did not realize, until this horrendous experience, that the Labia help with the prevention of vaginal and Urinary Tract infections. Evidently, the labia serve as a barrier to prevent various bacteria from sneaking in. Vaginal lips also help to guide urine in a straight line. I discovered this insight after continually peeing down my right leg or off the side of the toilet in every public restroom where I refused to sit on the germ-infested seat. Therefore, it was necessary to replace the missing lip. My prolapsed bladder was repaired with a hammock (a mesh cradle holding my bladder in place), and my uterus was removed due to severe infection. A large tumor was removed from an ovary. Yes - this was a complete overhaul to a very sensitive area. Perhaps a Cesarean Section would have been a better exit route?

Giving birth resulted in numerous changes to my body. I put myself through this extreme transformation two times; once vaginally and once via C-section. The resulting miracle of two beautiful daughters is definitely my Magnum Opus. Yet, I will find myself spending a life time ridding the evidence of giving birth that my body endured. Like most women, I will obsess on my frontal ponch, skin sag, hair loss, and stretch marks created by this remarkable process. I will cuss at the expansion of my hips and pout about my sagging tits. I will cry about my inability to enjoy sex the way I once did.

Comrades and Sisters, we all fuss about our aging appearance, especially during hormonal changes and after giving birth. It is a shame that we do this to ourselves instead of allowing our battle wounds to represent the true warriors that we are. I'm not promoting a "just let yourself go" approach, but I want to point out the unreasonable extent to which women continue to fret over appearance, even after nature performs its miracles. The fact that our bodies endure dramatic weight gain and hormonal changes in a such a short period of time is an ideal excuse for body imperfections. The idea that a head, damn near the size of a soccer ball, busts through a very small exit route leaves me wondering how we ever recover at all. But we do heal, forget, and often do it again. What extraordinary facilities we have!

By the way, with such a problematic birth, I neglected to inquire about the issue I was originally so worried about; pooping on the table. Two weeks after the birth of my daughter, I asked my husband about it. He dutifully told the truth. Yes, I had pooped…just a little. Turns out, I didn't care anymore.

Chapter 3

What Up? Hormones

Another fun, female experience of aging is the dramatic change in hormones. I've never given much attention to the concept of menopause. Other than the occasional moment when I witness a woman appearing to have just crawled out of an erupting volcano, fanning herself and declaring, "Don't mind me, I'm just having a hot flash," I don't remember ever discussing the issue with any menopausal woman. I find this incredibly weird, considering its impact. I've decided that women are much tougher than ever given credit for. The whole birthing process; we often get credit for that. But no one warns us or talks about the numerous challenges surrounding hormone changes, and it's pretty brutal.

My hormone story is both a familiar and peculiar one. It is a story I insist on sharing with other women because there is such valuable information to be learned from it.

A few years ago, I began to experience drastic mood swings. I would be very melancholy and unmotivated one day, and off the scale angry and irritable the next. Having never experienced "depression" before, my spouse would patiently explain to me that my brain chemicals must be off, resulting in the effects of depression. He should know, because he has battled this fate for years.

During this time, as a teacher, I had to put on a happy face and fake my misery. Evidently, I wasn't the best faker because a colleague of mine eventually told me that I should get my hormones checked. This really pissed me off!

My daughters were confused by my fluctuating state of anger and started referring to that side of me as "Tonya" (a not so nice reference to Tonya Harding, the infamous ice skater who collaborated a scheme to injure her competitor). I desperately tried to change my tune and fix what was happening inside of me. I started regulating my diet and exercise more carefully. I began to journal and meditate on a daily basis. I talked with a therapist. I started adding vitamins, probiotics, melatonin, and apple cider vinegar to my daily routine – as suggested by several female friends. Yet, my mood did not improve, and suddenly, I found myself gaining 15 pounds in 4 months! No wonder I was so damn depressed!

I finally went to the doctor; a most hated task of mine. Blood was drawn. Chit chat happened. I left the office with a prescription of anti-depressants. My God.

After eight weeks of anti-depressants, I was in worse shape than when I started. My therapist suggested switching to a different flavor of anti-depressant. So I did. Four weeks of that and I still wanted to murder someone. Therefore, I stopped taking everything and hauled my sorry ass into the OBGYN office and declared that I wasn't leaving until someone could tell me what was wrong. Finally, hormone tests were given.

The results came back and alarmed my doctor enough to call me while I was on vacation. She explained to me that my Testosterone levels were off the chart for a female. That's right...I had the attitude and sex drive of a 20-year-old male with a motorcycle and tiny dick. It didn't take long for us to realize why this was so. My husband was taking a prescription of Testosterone, applied as a lotion. Evidently, the hormone is transferrable through skin, clothing, and sheets. My husband, by seeking energy and a revitalized sex drive, was turning me into a man!

In hind sight, I should have suspected Testosterone. After all, my vagina had swollen to an unusual size, but I just figured that because I was gaining weight, my hooch was getting fat too. I dismissed all of the black hairs on my chin because I figured every aging woman grows a beard. I assumed that the balding spots on my forehead were due to all the damage I've done to my hair. I grew up in the 80's for Hell's sake! And the increase of giant underground zits, well, I blamed that on fast food.

Roughly three months after ridding my life of an overdose of testosterone, my hormone levels were tested again. Results concluded that I now had NO testosterone in my system, which I learned was not good for me either. Apparently, the overdose triggered my own system to quit making ANY testosterone. So, I left the office with a medley prescription of estrogen, progesterone, and testosterone.

The hormone therapy seemed to help, some. Yet, like most medications, one issue was exchanged for another. The quick ramble of possible side effects thrown in at the end of medication advertisements may seem laughable in the moment, but not so funny when you actually experience the unintended effects. With hormone replacements, my manly characteristics subsided but my female bits seemed enraged. My breasts became very tender and full, much like they felt with pregnancy. Migraines seemed to become more frequent. My temperament switched from anger to unfocused, and other unexplainable issues crept in. So, without a doctor's advice, I eventually quit taking all of it, except for the progesterone. By now, I had moved on to more pressing issues in my life. And the only reason I continued to take the progesterone is because I had read an article that suggested progesterone could help me lose weight. I was so desperate to get those damn last seven pounds off! It didn't work, of course.

Hormone changes are inevitable with age and can certainly be a factor in mood swings, weight gain, loss of energy, and sex drive. Strangely, the conversation about hormones is not a common one, nor is there much research or information surrounding female hormones. In fact, in my own research, I have discovered considerable conflicting information regarding hormones and hormone replacements. One certainty is, however, that for centuries, women have been under-represented and excluded from medical science. Most of our understanding regarding pain, sickness, and psychological irregularities comes from the perspective of men, based on the studies of men, and conducted by men.

Further, for centuries, doctors commonly diagnosed women with "hysteria." In Western Medicine, hysteria was considered a "mental disease" even though the symptoms were synonymous with those of normal female sexuality and hormone fluctuations. A woman may have been diagnosed as "hysterical" simply because she felt irritable, anxious, or emotional. Often times, the father or husband of the woman acting "hysterical" would insist on a treatment for their unruly behavior. Insane asylums and hysterectomies were common treatments for women diagnosed with "hysteria".

It's been approximately four years since my bout of "hysteria" and involuntary sex change. Yet I find myself back in the doctor's office to address more frustrating developments to my body. The most unfavorable change being my inability to get a good night's rest. Nightly hot flashes tend to keep me awake and temperature intolerant. Now in full-blown menopause, I have requested hormone replacement therapy - again. I was prescribed a low-dose of estrogen, in patch form, which has helped – somewhat – with my sleeping issues. I'm hoping that menopause and I will eventually come to a more friendly and balanced agreement.

After my hormonal showdown, I have vowed to teach my daughters about one of the most consequential components to female health. In Sex Education and Health courses, we are taught that hormones are involved in menstruation and reproduction which only encompasses limited information. And in social settings, the topic is often taboo. Women should have a better understanding of what their hormones are regulating in their bodies. They should also be aware of the fact that hormones continually change and can cause a multitude of mental and physical challenges. I don't want my daughters to feel ashamed about mood swings, unexplained weight gain, tender breasts, abnormal hair growth, acne, bloating, sleep irregularities, heavy menstrual cycles, or numerous other complications due to hormones. I don't want them to be misdiagnosed by a doctor who doesn't ask the right questions, give the right tests, or dismisses the severity of their issues.

In essence, women tend to be under-educated about their bodies, particularly hormones. We need to take charge of our own health and pay attention to our bodies' voice. The debate as to the accuracy of hormone testing as well as the benefits of hormone replacements will continue. There should be no debate, however, that hormone changes really suck and can have several life altering ramifications.

I simply wish that my husband and I had been alerted to the possible side effects that *his* hormone replacements caused (on the significant other). Additionally, I did not feel warned or prepared for the physical and mental changes that hormones contributed to as I aged. Had the conversations ever transpired between myself and the aging women in my life, perhaps I would have felt comfort in knowing that my issues were not simply psychological. Had I been better educated about hormones, I could have addressed my medical issues more timely and effectively and avoided feeling erratic. Perhaps I also could have dodged taking medications meant for other diagnoses.

I doubt that health education programs within schools will ever properly address the female anatomy. I'm not certain that hormone discussions and evaluations will be routinely or adequately addressed in most doctor's offices either. But I am convinced that women are innately in tune with their bodies and certainly want to have answers when the alarms sound. I am hopeful that women are starting to empower themselves by talking candidly about their experiences and doing their own research and analysis on hormones. Keep talking and teaching, warrior women. Let's help younger generations age without a blindfold.

Chapter 4

Self-Validation

There was time when I could teach dance all day and still feel like I could hit the night club that evening. But my mid 40's brought new challenges to my physical activity. First, recovery from a day of teaching dance became more grueling. I had to start regulating the intensity of my workouts, knowing that a "full out" day would require significant recovery time as well as a gut full of anti-inflammatories. Second, getting on and off the floor in a graceful manner became, well, less graceful. This reality is quite problematic for a dance teacher. Third, every jump and leap was accompanied by a squirt of pee. I found myself frequently apologizing to my students for pissing my pants in front of them.

I began to question my value as a dance teacher and was experiencing a tremendous amount of anxiety about the time I had left in my career. I watched my high school students flourish into beautiful dancers, envious of their abilities I once exhibited. I mentored young student-teachers with their ability to move with ease and hated them for it (just a little bit). I tried to adjust my teaching style to a more verbal approach, like many coaches do, but it didn't feel authentic or satisfying to me. I became incredibly critical of my looks as I stared in the mirror and compared myself to the youthful bodies and faces I stood beside.

The reality of aging was becoming more evident as I noticed differences in how people responded to me. I never thought I would miss having to show my ID to purchase alcohol or get into a club. But I do. I never thought I would miss the misogynistic whistle, cat call, or horn honk from random men on the street. But, oddly, I do. I never thought I would miss subtle flirting from colleagues and in public places. Indeed, I do.

I have had to find ways to self-validate and care less about the attention I may or may not receive from others. The ability to self-validate is a skill that is both challenging and rare. Most of us are taught to care about what others think and even attempt to prove ourselves worthy and likable. We get so much satisfaction from the validation that others give us. Our societies' obsession with social media supports this claim. It's alluring to be "liked," yet being "liked" can be so incredibly artificial and dangerous.

As a high school teacher, I was privy to the negative ramifications that social media was having on our society, most notably our teens. Back in the early 2000's, kids were discovering the numerous ways in which to connect with others through their devices. My students participated in the sprint to attractively brand themselves to compete in a most judgmental market. I watched my students change. They became much less interested in physical activity and more drawn to their screens by the day. They became less verbally communicative and attention spans were waning. I was most alarmed by the number of students who were increasingly being diagnosed with anxiety and depression.

I consoled students who experienced cyber bullying and I notified authorities when students were being victimize by cyber sexual predators. I watched the anxiety levels of students intensely increase as they recognized all the social engagements that they were being left out of. My students were incredibly consumed with and impacted by "the numbers"; how many followers and likes their accounts were receiving. The young women were especially obsessed with displaying the right image that could compare with their competitors. Photo editing became a necessary skill. I watched girls obsess about their body image; never feeling adequate. I witnessed the shame that came with discovering private images that had been shared with the world. I listened to numerous conversations of my students sharing information that was simply false and misleading, yet they insisted on its accuracy because their social media platform said so. I knew, many years ago, that these devices and the addictiveness of them would eventually be the demise of true human connection. Some fifteen plus years later, I contend that my early prediction is proving true.

Several studies between 2018 and 2021 reveal that teens are spending, on average, nine hours per day on social media platforms. Can you imagine what you would do with an extra nine hours per day? This number completely alarms and saddens me. Not only are the young, impressionable minds accumulating unaccredited information-overload, but they are engaging in an unhealthy sedentary lifestyle. All of the bells, vibrations, and alerts of our devices serve as an endless reminder to stay connected to a world that breeds anxiety and depression, particularly for teen girls.

It is no secret that our devices are designed to get and keep the users hooked. I find it incredibly telling that many Silicon Valley tech developers are raising their own children tech free because of their understanding of the negative effects of these devises. In fact, Bill Gates, founder of Microsoft, and Steve Jobs, Co-founder & CEO of Apple, had strict and limited access for their children to use the very devices they helped to create (CNBC, 2018).

Former Facebook executive, Chamath Palihapitiya, has recently spoken out about the harm that social networking is doing to civil society. Chamath says that he feels "tremendous guilt" about the company he helped develop. He further explained, "I think we have created tools that are ripping apart the social fabric of how society works" (CBS News, 2017).

Another Facebook executive, Frances Haugen, is known as the whistle-blower who revealed the findings of Facebook's own research. This research concluded that Facebook "amplifies hate, misinformation, and political unrest – but the company hides what it knows" (Time, 2022). Further, Instagram, owned by Facebook, is "harmful most particularly to teenage girls." Body image issues and suicidal thoughts were attributed to the use of Instagram. Frances explained that the algorithms used were designed to optimize user engagement and reaction. But its own research concludes that "content that is hateful, divisive, and polarizing dominates the information feed."

So, what in the hell does the negative effects of social media have to do with aging? Everything! Now, at such a young age, women are exposed to an infinite amount of information and imagery, most of which paints a very negative picture of aging. The amount of misinformation and misrepresentation is like never before. Opinions and life styles are being formed and driven by groups who desire to allure individuals into their camp or belief system. Accountability for this form of induction with all its untruths and unkindness is nonexistent. Further, the social media market is a thriving business. Not only are the platforms making an astronomical amount of money, but advertisers are able to target their audience and profit from tracking personal information. Females, in particular, are inundated with images, products, and remedies to help them be thin, young, and attractive. Unfortunately, most forms of media, define for women, what it is to be desirable. And that standard is hardly attainable.

It has only been in the most recent years that social media platforms have emerged in support of non-standard images for beauty and success. I get excited about a widened representation of women. The occasional silver haired model always captures my attention, but is often a lure to anti-aging products or some cliché' quote about being "old and sexy." As I try to grapple with the aging process, I realize that the mindset needed to combat a negative mentality will not be represented on most social media platforms. Therefore, I feel that one of our biggest opponents to redefining age is social media. And what a GIANT to have to battle.

The beauty of our current elderly generation is that they were not immersed into an era of technology that dominated their time. Unlike younger generations, older people seem to be able to unplug and disengage much easier. What a gift. Perhaps it is up to us, the maturing folk, to teach our children and grandchildren about life beyond the screen. It is the authentic, *lived* experiences that will provide them with the self-validation needed to bestow upon society the honest definition of growing into a healthy, happy, and beautiful human.

Chapter 5

The Enlightenment

Near the end of my hormone crisis; my transition from woman to man, then man to woman (Chapter 3), I was also experiencing another major life upheaval. My spouse, an attorney, decided that it was time in his career to make a change. I was also feeling stagnant and insecure in my career and thought that the change sounded like an opportunity. So, we left our home state of Utah, leaving behind a 20-year-old daughter, aging parents, friends, jobs, and a home we loved. Off to the great state of Colorado; to a small town in the mountains, without a mall.

Putting a hard-working, busy body, socialite into a town without a job or a familiar face is like putting a teen in a room without internet service. Survivable, yes, but terrifying as hell. I felt that my personality and energy level may be unmatched for this slow and quiet place.

My husband landed a fantastic job and quickly made friends within his work environment. My youngest daughter,

15 years old at the time, was also filling her days, although a bit reluctantly, with school, clubs, homework, and new friends. As for me, I mostly percolated. For the first time in my life, my mind was still. I found myself in the mountains, on trails, lakes, and rivers observing my new and peaceful surroundings.

Never before had I been so observant of nature. I noticed the abundant sounds of birds and bugs. As I wandered down the river banks and hiked up mountain trails, the birds made me feel like they were including me in their conversations . I named the birds according to their color (e.g. Black-Blue-Tail, Yellow Face, etc.), disregarding their scientific names knowing that I would never remember those. The rivers and streams captivated my attention for crazy amounts of time. I could actually hold still and disappear in senseless thought for hours. The perpetual flow of the water, for some reason, gave me a bit of anxiety. I suppose it's because the rush of the water seemed endless, never taking a rest, and the thought of life without an end seemed unnatural and daunting. So, I would close my eyes and beg the reverent sound of endlessness to pacify my nerves. The constant rustling of the bushes, kept my defense senses on full alert. I kept expecting to be ambushed by a critter.

I saw deer quite often, yet every time I did, I was excited and grateful for their presence. But the geese were my favorite animal to see and hear. Not only did I find the goose to be so beautiful, but I was fascinated with their social behaviors. I love that geese routinely change formation to offer leadership to those in the front of the V as well as a bit of rest from breaking wind to those in the back. Geese also take care of one another. When one goose falls behind, other geese in the flock will offer company and assistance. Geese have a strong presence in flight and on ground. Their monolithic size for a bird of flight is majestic and impressive. The geese exhibit an audible language that is direct, confident, and amusing. In fact, when I hear the geese honking, I immediately stop and give them my full attention and praise.

I also noticed the sound of silence. Erie at first, the lack of noise when sitting atop a mountain or next to a still lake can be gratifying and spiritual. The light was even quiet here. It's been a long time since I could stare at the night sky and identify the big dipper. I felt lucky.

I decided that I really wanted to see a bear... no I didn't... yes I did. I just didn't want the bear to see me or my bear snack of a dog, Mr. Fred Rogers. Point being, I was discovering how much I loved the outdoors, observing animals, and experiencing my newfound sparkle as well as a calm energy I never knew existed inside of me. I had no doubt that the hustle and bustle of my life back in Salt Lake City would have never afforded me this level of peace.

My time on the trails had introduced me to more than just nature. I met many inspirational people. Unfortunately, they may never know the impact they had on me.

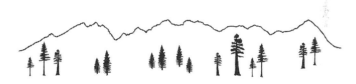

My Trail-Mates

My first encounter with a trail-mate almost ended badly. Rich, a man in his 70's (I'm guessing) with a tall, slim figure and kind smile passed me on trails quite often. One day, he began telling me about some lesser known trails that he liked to venture on. During our conversation,

I shared with him that I was new to town and appreciated the hiking tips. Certainly, with good intention, Rich invited me to join the "Senior Hikers Club." That's right. Even when I asked him to repeat the club name, the word "senior" jumped out at me like a threatened rattlesnake. It bit me with the kind of paralyzing venom that causes one to lose focus and all comprehension. When I got back to my car, I couldn't wait to text my husband to inform him that it was definitely time for that facelift. As I was texting, Rich startled me when he knocked on my driver side window. I cracked the window and he apologetically explained that he knew I wasn't a senior, but thought that this spritely group would be a great way to find new friends with similar interests. He must have noticed the horrified look on my face when the word "senior" came out of his mouth. For the first time, I understood that I may have graduated to a new age category that came with negative labels. Needless to say, I nonsensically became paranoid of a word used to describe people who are NOT young. I have no doubt that the Senior Hikers Club would kick my ass at any physical endeavor. But maybe they would let me join under the name "Junior member" for the sake of my vanity.

On another day, same trail, I happened upon two women and their dogs. As I stepped off the trail to let them pass, the Saint Bernard accompanying his master and her twin sister, abruptly stopped and began to lean heavily into me. The woman approached me and gently put her arm on my shoulder and asked if I was terminally ill. When I told her no, she asked if I was in any pain. Any pain? This seemed like a trick question. In my hesitation and confusion to answer, she began to explain that her dog was a trained service dog who was detecting my pain. The best I could give her was that I had arthritis and might be a little screwy in the head. The conversation continued and I learned that the twins had just celebrated their 77th birthday and had recently hiked approximately 50 miles on the Colorado trail with their grandson. Yup, these "elderly" women with their heavy backpacks spent days doing an activity that I couldn't fathom doing at 51. I think about the twins often. Any time I catch myself using my age as an excuse not to do an activity, I remind myself that the twins would scoff at my reluctance. By the way, the following day, I made an appointment for a full medical exam, just in case Buddy the dog was on to something. Fortunately, he was wrong. I'm basically healthy.

Another hike, different trail, gave me the pleasure to meet another older woman, Lydia, and her furry mate. She came upon my dog, Fred, and me at the trailhead as I stood staring at the slope and contemplating the hike. She inquired as to who we were because she had never seen us before, on the trail that she hiked daily. After brief introductions, I asked her if the trail was difficult. She looked at me with bewilderment and asked, "Difficult for who?" I felt I had to explain that I was an "inexperienced hiker" and was still getting used to the high altitude. She smiled and replied, "You just take one step at a time." I giggled out of embarrassment. She continued, "The great thing is, when you are ready, you simply stop and descend."

My hell! She made it sound so simple. I doubt that Lydia had any idea that her words would be on my mind indefinitely and would help define the moment when I understood that my fear of so many challenges arose from my tunnel vision as to the intimidating task ahead of me. I stood at the trailhead and could only see the steep terrain and mountain top. Yet, Lydia wanted me to see the smaller and more profound steps along the way. She wanted me to notice the variety of trees and wild flowers. Lydia hoped I would appreciate the differing views from various rest points. She wanted me to stop for shade and water and to listen to nature's songs. She expected me to feel empowered with my abilities to make decisions as to my own path.

I have been scared to age, not knowing what awaits me. I have been overwhelmed with the idea of a difficult climb and inevitable finish. I certainly did not recognize that I had some control and choice over what my hike would offer and when I was ready to descend. How lucky I was to have conversed with Lydia on this morning. Her simple words of wisdom about hiking a challenging trail deeply resonated with me. It may be a stretch, but I concluded that I was absolutely meant to hear these words: Difficult for Who?, One Step at a Time, and Descend When You're Ready." Ultimately, my approach and definition of aging has become less daunting and much more exciting. And, YES, I slayed the fucking trail that day!

Perhaps the right people had to cross my path at a time when I was ready to pay attention. These trail-mates lightly reminded me that I am a woman in a maturing body, who was in desperate need a new map. They inspired me to create a new aging scenario. Their wisdom and example was the motivation I needed to explore a healthier aging psychology. I knew that I was not alone in thoughts, fears, and desires. Therefore, it was time for me to redefine the aging process and share my revelations with all my future trail-mates.

Chapter 6

Redefining Myself

As we age, we arrive at new junctures that bring forth change and revision to our thinking and behavior. In our younger years, change is more subtle and often worthy of celebration. My 16th birthday gave me the freedom of mobilization. Age 21 finally legalized my love of wine. Late in my 20's, I became a thriving adult with a new career, medical benefits, a mortgage, and a baby. My 30's were dominated by my career as well as full-blown motherhood. Reaching my early 40's denoted a time of intense focus on my financial stability as well as my sexual revolution.

My late 40's, however, snuck in and slapped me upside the head like no other age had done. Changes were no longer delicate. Instead, I woke up every day, ready to battle the next new challenge that Father Time presented. My Nana used to say, "Aging isn't for sissy's" and by damn, she was right!

As my own career as a dance teacher came to a close, I found myself flailing about; trying to figure out who and what I should be. Starting a new career at age 51 felt overwhelming. I pondered going back to school to get a degree in a completely different area; something less physical. Then I would remind myself that I just finished paying off my graduate school loans a mere eight years ago. Further, when I did the math, I figured that another degree would really only give me approximately twelve years to work before my ideal retirement age of 65. Therefore, school did not feel like the wisest economic plan.

On the other hand, I found myself frustrated with other job options such as part-time or those that did not require a specific degree. The hourly pay was simply not acceptable to me, especially considering that I had worked my ass off to obtain a Master's Degree. Why we continue to debate the necessity of a standard livable wage in this country is inconceivable.

While I fretted over a possible new career, I also found myself struggling with another identity crises. My oldest daughter, Sawyer, yes, the one who ripped my vagina off (Chapter 2), moved out from under my supervision at 18 years of age. Off she went to start a life of her own. As a mama, I should feel proud of this act of independence. Of course, I was proud but also felt a weird sense of abandonment. No longer would I have a daily influence on my daughter and my role as "mom" suddenly changed. I did not like this feeling. I knew it wouldn't be long before my younger daughter, Amelia, would follow suit and ultimately leave my husband and I "empty nesters."

I always imagined the moment when my husband and I would be back to our duet, having raised our daughters to full independence. I featured us behaving as we did in our youth... a bit rowdy. I figured we would be cooking and cleaning in the nude and doing whatever in the hell we wanted without interruptions or judgement. The stereo would blast *our* tunes and we would never have to watch a Disney movie again! There would be no more late nights, waiting for a kid to get home safely. No longer would we need to manage chores and bitch about an untidy house. Editing papers and assisting with homework assignments would cease. No longer would we be running to and from school, dance, and Martial Art events. We could go out to dinner for half the price and engage in adult conversations. We could be intimate without tiptoeing, locking doors, and blasting classical music. Yet, once the nest emptied, my reality was not what I had imagined.

Certainly, there is some excitement in change. The end of a career and "motherhood" as we define it, can afford the much-needed time we always seem to be short on. It can offer new adventures and goals as well as serve as an opportunity for a fresh start. But this change in role definition can also bring sadness and a sense of loss. The melancholy I felt about the end of a career and the vacancy in my home was a little unexpected. Yet, the sadness felt a bit irrational considering that my goal was always to retire from a career before it retired me as well as raise my kids to full independence. But it hurt nonetheless.

With children raised and a successful career behind me, I noticed that my life spun at a much slower pace; a gratifying, needed, yet unfamiliar speed. As I contemplated and prepared for my next segment, I realized that moving forward must be accompanied by an acceptance that I will have new roles and purposes. I suppose it is not about changing who I am, but *adapting* to my new circumstances. If I can find definition in an older me, perhaps I can free myself from the burden of maintaining a false youthfulness. Finding acceptance in my older self may relieve me from the sadness of what I have lost with age. Perhaps I can let go of continuously seeking products and procedures to change my age and release the pressure of looking and behaving in the ways that society unrealistically expects me to. This sounds rational, but easier said than done.

We expend a great deal of time and energy perfecting the roles we take on. Daughter, sibling, friend, wife, mother, artist, teacher... whatever your roles may be, there will come a day when you must adapt. It's easy to get attached or even stuck on roles, and when we are forced to change them, we find ourselves grieving their loss. It is okay to express sadness over changing roles for that is evidence that you took pride in your title. But being "stuck" there is a problem. Remind yourself that you don't ever forfeit your hard-earned title, you simply rewrite your job description.

In addition to role adaption, as we age we will be faced with the challenge of adjusting our routines, hobbies, and activities. Too often, aging seniors surrender to the idea that their age, their number in years, is reason enough to abandon once enjoyed activities. So often, I hear seniors declare, "Not at my age." I watch my parents gradually give up on their cherished activities as their minds and bodies don't allow the execution they are accustomed to. Out of frustration, they simply surrender. Sometimes it's easier to *not* perform the skill any more than be reminded of increasing limitations. I suppose I threw in the white flag of surrender when my dance teaching career continuously reminded me that I was losing my abilities to age. It has taken a change in the expectations that I place on myself for me to enjoy the artform I have always loved. After two years of concealing my artistry due to my growing physical limitations, I have learned to dance simply for the joy that it brings me. Oddly, it took time for me to realize that I could dance without having to teach it. This adaption in both mindset and activity has allowed me to rediscover a relationship with by body and movement that I find so gratifying and judgement-free (maybe because now I dance in the privacy of my living room).

It is important to acknowledge the inadequacies, adjust the mindset, and discover new ways to perform and/or partake in loved activities. For example, there is no need to walk a mile; walk a block. No need to paint a picture for public display; paint one for yourself. No need to fumble with small car model parts or jewelry; have your grandkid assist you. No need to give up cooking; invite a friend or family member over and be their sous chef. No need to stop being intimate with your partner; explore other ways to be affectionate under the sheets. No need to grand jete' into the air to dance; turn on your tunes and authentically move the way your body can.

It may be necessary for the elderly to ask for support and assistance with their activities. Simply asking for help is difficult for so many seniors. Not only is their pride at stake, but they may not want to "bother" others with their request. Many seniors think that by asking for help, they are revealing their weaknesses and inadequacies. It is critical that we have the conversations with our senior loved ones regarding the need to *adapt* to new ways of doing tasks and activities as well as accept help from others.

In this next phase of my life, I anticipate transitioning my primary concerns from my adult children to my parents. Now in their 70's, health issues have become a worry. With an approximate life expectancy in the United States to be 81.4 for women and 75.1 for men (Vital Statistics Rapid Release, CDC, 2020), I have some angst about the time I have left with my parents. I also wonder if they will need assistance with basic living and who may end up with the responsibility of caring for them. I worry about the affordability of caring for my parents. These issues haunt so many Americans. Oddly, we don't talk much about it. In fact, I have no idea what my parents have in mind for their grand finale. It feels morbid to bring it up, so I don't. I have asked a few basic questions like "urn or casket?" but have yet to get a final answer. They are still deciding.

Part Two – Our Story

"Old age is not a disease – it is a strength and survivorship, triumph over all kinds of vicissitudes and disappointments, trials, and illnesses."

~ Maggie Kuhn, Ageism Activist

Chapter 7

Ageism

Some of my grief about the loss of the more youthful me comes from the realization that I no longer see myself as desirable to others. In social situations, I find myself scanning the room for female competitors and unfairly judging the women who look younger and more fuckable. Most aging women are fully aware that our generational status keeps us low on the desirability scale. Even in situations where I appear confident and fierce, I often feel dismissed and invisible. I don't remember feeling this way in my younger years. My audience, once attentive, has recognized my age.

In my younger years, I didn't think much about Ageism as a category of discrimination; at least not with the same sensitivity I had for other "isms" such as racism and sexism. But now as I progress into the category of an aging woman, I am discovering the weight and impact such judgements can have. I don't wish to be lumped into any group that may suggest inferiority simply because –

Unlike many countries, America has a weak system in place to support our aging population. According to the US Census Bureau as well as the United Health Foundation, in 2021 approximately 16.5% of the population were age 65 and older. It is estimated that by the year 2030, 1 in 5 Americans will be of retirement age. This means that for the first time in U.S. history, the elderly (65 +) are projected to outnumber children. Not only can this shift in population catapult our society into a financial crisis, but may force us to address our society's battle with ageism.

Systemic ageism is the practice of stereotyping or discrimination against people simply because of their age, just as racism and sexism procure with skin color and gender. I will address three types of systemic ageism: (1) **Institutional Ageism**, which occurs when an institution perpetuates ageism through its actions and policies, (2) **Interpersonal Ageism**, which occurs in social interactions, and (3) **Internalized Ageism**, which is when a person internalizes negative ageist beliefs and applies them to themselves.

Institutional Ageism

When it comes to consideration for hiring, promotions, pay raises, or other advancing opportunities, ageism is often practiced institutionally. About 3 in 5 workers have witnessed or experienced age discrimination in the workplace (AARP, 2019). Further, many aging workers suggest that they were pushed out of their work environment because of the negative stereotypes about older employees. There exists many damaging assumptions about older employees including the idea that they can no longer contribute fresh and innovative ideas. Many employers also feel that older workers maintain a slower pace at work, which has never been proven to be true in any accredited study. These unrealistic views of older employees being incapable, dull, or outperformed is one of the reasons we see widespread ageism in the work force.

Ageist stereotypes contribute to the lack of hiring workers over the age of 50. In fact, the online process of applying for a job has allowed companies to privately instill specific algorithms to weed out certain candidates. For example, if one were to list age, birthdate, or school graduation dates, the algorithm may bypass a particular applicant out of hiring consideration. Many companies have a standard of hiring for the "long haul" meaning they will only invest in individuals that they would expect to be with the company for many years. If over 50, the employer assumes that retirement of this individual is just around the corner, therefore, she/he won't be invested for the long term. Additionally, employers tend to think that hiring a young individual will give them the opportunity to mold and train someone who will be with the company for years to come. This philosophy is flawed, however. Studies show that as people get older, they change jobs less frequently. Between the ages of 18-24, people change jobs an average of 5.7 times. By the time a person reaches ages 45-51, they are only likely to change jobs 1.9 times (Apollo Technical, 2022 & GoRemotely, Domovski, 2022).

At age 51 with a Master's degree in Teaching, I am frustrated with the challenges I am having as I seek new employment. After being turned down from numerous jobs, I sought professional advice. My resume was reviewed by three different sources and all of them suggested that I take the dates out of my resume because my potential employer may not be interested in hiring someone my age. For years I have adhered to the philosophy that 50 is the new 30. But I have discovered that being a half century old is not always appreciated in the job market (or many facets of life, for that matter). Evidently, my age puts me in the 'less desirable employee' category. Contributing to the confusion of ageism in employment is the fact that I have had several conversations with employers who claim that older workers are much more reliable and detail oriented than those of younger generations. Whether this argument is fact or opinion, I do not know. I am simply amazed at how one's value in the workforce is often determined by age.

Ageism in the workforce is difficult to prove so it is often ignored. What can't be ignored, however, is that several institutions have written policies in place that can be considered an act of ageism. Hiring practices, advancement opportunities, and retirement policies often reek with institutional ageism. Interesting examples of ageist practices are seen in forced retirement. For instance, air traffic controllers have a mandatory retirement age of 56. Federally employed law enforcement officers must retire at age 57. The age for pilots and foreign service officers to mandatorily leave their career is 65. Judges also have a required retirement age, depending on the state they serve.

The practice of a mandatory retirement age supports the theory that motor skills, judgement, and overall physical vitality diminishes with age. This rationale is certainly warranted, but seems to dismiss the individualized aging process and the varying degrees to which a person declines physically and cognitively. Forced retirement by age, as well as other systemic ageism practices, neglect the fact that senior employees possess a depth of knowledge and experience that can benefit their company. Further, older workers carry a maturity level that can benefit employee culture. Companies that regard senior workers as mentors and loyalists understand the value of possessing "intellectual property."

The inability to retire when needing or wanting to also poses an entirely different and troublesome issue. Approximately 29% of US households headed by someone age 55 or older have no retirement savings or pension, meaning they will have to continue working or rely solely on Social Security (AARP, Gibson, 2019), which forces far too many seniors into low income or poverty. The Social Security program was designed to help economically sustain our aging population, however it was never meant to be the only household income. The benefits are designed to provide 40% of one's pre-retirement income. Furthermore, cost of living adjustments in the social security program are well below the pace of inflation.

Adding concern is the fact that many seniors will face increasing health and medical challenges and may possibly require assistance for daily needs. There is a significant financial burden to hire In-Home Care services or place a loved one in Assisted Living or a Nursing Home. In 2020, the median cost for Assisted Living in the United States was $4,300 per month (Senior Living, 2022). This amount varies among states and facilities but provides a reality that may not have been realized. Yet politicians continue to debate and threaten the sustainability of Medicare and Social Security benefits and often manage to cut or reduce various programs to help senior citizens in their daily lives. The government, nor most private citizens, have properly planned for the new reality of living longer.

Several years ago, my grandparents had to be placed into an Assisted Living Center. I never imagined how difficult this would be. They lived in a lovely middle-class home that they proudly built together. They were collectors of antique vehicles, classic china, model cars, vintage clothing, and a variety of other dated possessions. Having lived through The Depression, they also held onto unnecessary items such as old pillows, magazines, grocery sacks, paperwork, and most any item brought into their home over a span of 40 years. Their yard was also an area of personal fulfillment with rock walls and a designer car-shop built by Papa and flower gardens routinely cared for by Nana. It was a comfortable place to live and they were proud of all that their home represented.

When the decision had to be made to get Nana and Papa better and more consistent care, we took on the overwhelming task of downsizing from an approximately 3200 square foot house and a four-car garage to a small, one-bedroom apartment with a kitchenette. Never mind the amount of physical work it took to complete this undertaking, the emotional toll on everyone involved was absolutely heart breaking. To discard Nana and Papa's "stuff" or "possessions," was taking from them a lifetime of "memories" and "pride". To move two individuals from a comfortable home to a less private place shared with so many other aging people tested their dignity. We witnessed our loved ones reluctantly accept their new environment; one that never seemed to completely belong to them. Although our family was relieved to have 24-hour care for Nana & Papa, we will never forget the sacrifices they endured in order to live for as long as their heartbeats intended.

Our family was lucky to have found an Assisted Living Center that was clean, aesthetically appealing, well-staffed, and well-managed. We were also fortunate that our loved ones had the financial means to receive this type of favorable care. Unfortunately, not all aging centers provide the quality care and atmosphere one would hope for. The difference primarily extends from a culture where one's socioeconomic status determines the care they will receive. Further, it is difficult to regulate the facilities where aging and disabled care are being provided. Random facility checks, which are often pre-scheduled and facility oriented (rather than resident-based) seem to only touch the surface of what should be a quality standard of living for our elderly population.

Through my experiences with care facilities, I have witnessed concerning issues like low staffing, employee turnover, underpaid staff, lack of training, deteriorating infrastructure, mismanaged medications, and even abusive treatment. My strong recommendation prior to in-home care or placing a loved one in a facility is to be thorough in your search. Spend several hours in the facility and with the staff as an observer. Do so on different days with varying staff members. Check the cleanliness. Ask about the ratio between staff and residents. Investigate the daily routines of those living in the facility and note whether or not they are getting adequate exercise and socialization. Inquire about medication disbursement and monitor the accuracy of the dosage. Many residents will endure pain and discomfort that could easily be reduced with the proper medications. Likewise, residents are often over-medicated, particularly those in Memory Care, so that they are less of a burden to staff. Most importantly, once you have decided on the care center or home help, remain involved and visit frequently. Your visits may help reveal a difference between what is advertised about the facility or service and what actually takes place. Your consistent involvement will be the primary factor in the health and happiness of your loved one. Finally, I recommend that you associate yourself with various support groups that can assist *you* in having the best experience possible.

If placed in the proper facility, the environment can prove to be incredibly beneficial to your loved one's health. Not only can assistance with daily tasks be a relief to all, but the social life within a facility can provide the needed support necessary for good mental health. Having an active social life and feeling a sense of community will make a profound difference in healthy aging. I must also note that although I witnessed some of the ugly circumstances of Assisted Living, I also observed many tender moments between staff members and residents. As in any line of work, there are dedicated superstars who make all the difference.

Interpersonal Ageism

Unlike other cultures, here in the United States, we tend to view the elderly as inferior to youth. We have not instilled a sense of respect and value for our aging population. In Native American Culture, elders are looked upon as "Wisdom Keepers" and are treated with honor. In several Asian cultures, the elderly are dignified and families feel a sense of noble duty to care for aging parents and grandparents. In Greek Culture, old age is revered and celebrated, and respect for elders is central to the family.

In our society, we treat the elderly as though they were a burden. Most American families do not have aging parents in the home, nor do they have a plan in place to care for them. The American culture simply maintains negative views of the elderly, including unflattering labels and definitions. The language we use to describe our elderly has had a significant impact on their treatment and self-worth. Many words that come to mind include: stubborn, burned out, slow, dated, ornery, senile, crazy, weak, frail, tired, saggy, deaf, blind, old-fashioned, and difficult. Words are incredibly influential and define who and what we are. It is no surprise that the older we get, the less dignified and valuable we feel.

There are multiple examples of social interactions that manifest ageism. One destructive yet popular trend involves the act of scamming. Seniors are the target group for a various telephone, internet, and merchandise scams. Taking advantage of seniors is a growing concern as private information is more readily accessible to the perpetrators. Seniors are often preyed upon simply because they tend to be more trusting and may not have the proficiency to self-investigate the legitimacy of the ploy. Many scams lead the senior down an intentionally complicated path in order to create confusion. Seniors will often blame their aging mind for the lack of logic in the scam and will concede to the transaction simply to avoid appearing rude or unintelligent.

The media plays a significant role in Interpersonal Ageism. In an era of constant news and entertainment feed, people are more influenced by the screen than most any other entity. Religion, family, and education once played a more profound role in how people viewed themselves and the world. But the availability and relentlessness of the media has swung the pendulum. Images of glamour and success belong to the young and beautiful. Advertisers take advantage of the push for youth by inundating screens with their age defying products. Hollywood is also obsessed with youth, particularly for women. In the film industry, female actors often plateau by the time they reach 30 years of age. At this point, their careers slow and the number of available roles diminish as they approach middle age. This negative stigma of aging creates a mindset that women lose their looks and sex appeal a mere 5 years after full brain development (which is approximately age 25). In comparison, the roles for aging men are much more abundant. A man can be sexy in his 60's. The James Bond persona is a perfect example of sexist ageism. It is "normal" for viewers to see a man intimately involved with a much younger woman. The opposite relationship (an older woman with a younger man) is considered odd and simply doesn't sit right in the minds of most viewers.

Ageism is also widespread in healthcare. Discrimination, lower quality care, and misdiagnoses are more common among the elderly due to the preconceived notion that complaints of illness or injury are most likely a component of expected decline instead of a treatable issue. Many serious medical issues go undetected because physicians are reluctant to investigate further when the patient is already in a state of deterioration. Additionally, many intrusive treatments for severe illnesses are forgone due to the expected life-span of the patient (Senior Living, Hoyt, 2022). In other words, if they are on their way out, why bother?

The medical field, assisted living facilities, and the general public, regularly use a type of speech with the elderly that is a form of ageism. "Elderspeak" which involves talking to older adults using the oversimplified language, terms of endearment, or rhythmic tone of voice a person might use for a child is just another common way that ageism manifests in our society (Verywellhealth, Heerema, 2020). Elderspeak can unintentionally presume that the elder is incompetent and/or helpless. No adult likes being spoken to as though they were a child.

Internalized Ageism

It is human nature to internalize the beliefs that we are constantly fed and apply them to our own ideology and behavior. Internalized Ageism propagates much like a self-fulfilling prophecy, which is a prediction that by being *voiced* will come true. A continual diet of negative stereotypes will shape the minds and behavior of those being categorized as such. If our society fails to validate and respect the elderly , it will certainly marginalize an entire population and create an island of illegitimates; modern lepers, if you will.

The natural path of aging often leads to a much smaller world. The elderly often find themselves socially isolated and lonely, which can prompt depression. A world of isolation is one in which an individual feels unneeded. The consequential effects of feeling invisible are devastating to the body and tend to speed the natural decline. Additionally, the elderly are often accompanied by a multitude of medications to treat aging issues. But prescriptions have side effects and are often unproperly mixed with other medications and create havoc on the body and may increase feelings of anxiety and depression.

The passing of loved ones becomes a regular occurrence for the elderly; parents, siblings, friends, and neighbors disappear from lives. Grieving their loss is both a lonely and heavy burden to carry. The passing of loved ones also serves as a reminder that their own expiration date is nearing.

The natural changes that occur with aging are difficult enough to endure. The way in which we are treated in society may provide the first clues that the descent has begun. The ending of a career, the change in vital roles, and the exclusion from a fast-paced world will certainly lead one to question their current purpose and value. With age, the world may shrink and change, yet the fact remains, it is vital to feel purpose. The body must keep moving. The mind must stay active. The heart must remain socially engaged and connected. These needs are not just for one's happiness, but for one's survival.

Summary

Ageism is a form of inequity that affects everybody. Education, policy change, and intergenerational appreciation and respect are necessary to combat Ageism. We need to learn to understand and value the older generations and offer more positive representations of them, if for no other reason than, one day (if not already), we will be them.

Chapter 8

Aging of the Mind

My spouse and I have decided to team up and assist each other to function on a daily basis. We help each other remember names and words that have somehow escaped the memory bank. We often scramble to help the other find his/her cell phone, glasses, keys, and a million other misplaced items. We even help each other to drive. I regularly remind my husband that red means stop and that he must look behind him when backing up the vehicle. The loud and alarming bump strips on the road help me clue my husband in that he must drive within the lines. Likewise, my husband helps me to remember that I am operating a vehicle and should not be engaged in any conversation because evidently, I can no longer talk and drive simultaneously.

When having conversations, we no longer talk over televisions, music, dogs, or other distractions. We have to prepare the room with complete silence so that we can communicate without experiencing brain chaos. We also help each other to remember the details of previous conversations that may explain frequent confused looks on our faces.

We try, and sometimes fail, to remind each other of important dates, like birthdays and appointments. My husband is permanently scarred over forgetting our daughter's 21st birthday. I had left town to go spend time with her on this special occasion. One would think that the empty pillow next him would have been the reminder he needed to call and wish her a happy birthday, but it did not. I bought my spouse a satchel (man-purse) to store all the belongings he needed to take to work that were continuously left behind. But this remedy proved pointless because he would often leave for work and the satchel would not.

My husband is not alone in cognition decline; my memory is also increasingly challenged. Word recall is a daily frustration. If I pause mid-sentence for long enough, someone in the room eventually finds the missing word for me. And when they do, I'm generally irritated that the word belonged to my elementary years' vocabulary. I have had to ask my kids to simply respond to whatever name I call them because I regularly name swap without realizing it. Sometimes my forgetfulness makes me look like a dumb ass. I recently had to reschedule an appointment to get my tires changed; not once, not twice, but three times in one week! I brought the employees of the car-shop a box of donuts and offered no other excuse than I simply forgot to show up – 3 times.

I realize that my spouse and I are experiencing the natural decline in brain functioning that occurs with age. It is frustrating and sometimes depressing. We partake in many of the suggested tricks and remedies for keeping our brains sharp like supplements, brain games, meditation, and regular exercise. We like to believe that these defenses are helping. Nevertheless, we know that the decline in brain function, albeit slow, is already underway.

I remember, as a child, the "C" word was the scariest diagnosis one could get. No joke, Cancer of any kind is a devastating prognosis. But as an adult, and having watched numerous families suffer from Dementia, I am adding the "D" word to my list of greatest fears. Losing one's mind is about the cruelest disease imaginable.

As we age, our cognitive abilities naturally decline. More specifically, the skills that we tend to lose include memory, executive functions (e.g. flexible thinking & self-control), processing speed, reasoning, and multi-tasking. Fortunately, our brains naturally tend to improve in the areas of wisdom, expertise, and emotional maturity. How fast and severe one experiences cognitive decline varies significantly, and we don't have much evidence to explain the differences. However, over the last 25 years, we have learned a great deal more about the aging brain and have identified causes, risk factors, and some treatments for Dementia.

Dementia is a term we use to describe loss of memory and other cognitive functions that are severe enough to interfere with daily life. To be clear, Dementia is not the "normal" cognitive decline we experience with aging. Someone with Dementia has experienced abnormal brain change in which damaged brain cells are unable to properly communicate. Dementia is not a single disease, but an overall term that covers a wide range of specific medical conditions. Alzheimer's is one of these medical conditions and comprises approximately 70% of Dementia diagnoses (CDC, 2022). Alzheimer's is also the most progressive form of Dementia. Unfortunately, most abnormal changes that occur in the brain are permanent and will worsen over time.

Being diagnosed with Dementia is complicated. There is no one test to determine if someone has Dementia or how far along the disease has progressed. Instead, doctors consider a multitude of factors to determine whether someone may be suffering from Dementia and how far along they may be in the process. Doctors often rely heavily on the description of behavior from the patient and close family members to determine if Dementia may be an issue. Multiple neurological exams, diagnostic tests, and brain imaging may be administered to determine cognitive functions.

According to the Alzheimer's Association, those who have a parent or sibling with Alzheimer's are more likely to develop the disease than those who do not have a first-line relative with Alzheimer's. Those who have more than one first-line relative with Alzheimer's are at an even higher risk. Further, the risk of developing Dementia increases with age, especially after 65. Women are twice as likely to develop Dementia than men. Minorities are also at a higher risk of developing Dementia, particularly African American and Hispanic women. These populations have less access to quality healthcare and tend to have health conditions such as heart disease and diabetes which may play a role in the onset of Dementia (Alzheimer's Association, 2022).

The Alzheimer's Association and The Mayo Clinic list similar common **symptoms** of Dementia which include:

- Memory loss, often noticed by others
- Difficulty communicating or finding words
- Difficulty with visual and spatial abilities such as getting lost while driving
- Difficulty reasoning or problem-solving
- Difficulty handling complex tasks

- Difficulty planning and organizing
- Difficulty with coordination and motor skills
- Confusion & Disorientation.

Some of the **psychological signs** of Dementia may include:

- Personality changes
- Depression
- Anxiety
- Inappropriate Behavior
- Paranoia
- Agitation
- Hallucinations

While age, genetics, and family history may be factors for developing Dementia, there are many **risk factors** that people *can* control in order to lower their risk and even slow the disease:

- **Exercise**
  A multitude of diseases and illnesses are associated with a sedentary life style. Dementia is no exception. Lack of exercise is detrimental to overall brain function.
- **Diet**
  Research indicates a greater incidence of dementia in people who eat an unhealthy diet compared to those who follow a healthy diet. The Mediterranean diet which is rich in produce, whole grains, nuts, and seeds has shown to be the one of the most effective diets for cognitive health (Alzheimer's Association, 2022).
- **Excessive alcohol use**
  Alcohol causes changes in the brain. Excessive use has been linked to an increased risk of dementia. Women who consume eight or more drinks per week are considered excessive drinkers. And for men,

excess is defined as 15 or more drinks a week. A "drink" is defined as 5 ounces of wine or 12 ounces of beer. Therefore, according to several United States polls, 1 in 3 adults who drink alcohol are considered to be excessive users.

- **Cardiovascular risk factors**
  A person is at greater risk for Dementia if they have high blood pressure, high cholesterol, buildup of fats in artery walls, and/or obesity.
- **Depression**
- **Diabetes**
- **Smoking**
- **Air Pollution**
- **Head Trauma**
- **Sleep Disturbance**
  People who lack sleep or have sleeping disorders such as Sleep Apnea are at a higher risk for developing Dementia.
- **Vitamin and nutritional deficiencies**
  Low levels of Vitamin D, Vitamin B-6, Vitamin B-12 and Folate can increase risk of Dementia.
- **Medications that affect memory**
  Avoid long term use of over-the-counter sleep aids that contain Diphenhydramine and medications used to treat urinary urgency such as Oxybutynin. These medications have brain altering affects that may increase risk for Dementia (Medical News Today, 2015; AARP, 2019; Alzheimersdisease.net, 2020).

There is no bulletproof method for preventing Dementia. However, based on the risk factors listed above, it would be beneficial to take the necessary steps to avoid being at a high risk. Simply by maintaining a healthy diet and being physically active on a daily basis may help prevent numerous health issues including Dementia and Cardiovascular health. Keeping your mind active may delay the onset of Dementia as well as decrease its effects.

Smoking and excessive alcohol use should be reduced or eliminated. Ensure that you are properly treating any vitamin deficiencies. Practice good sleep methods to aid in the quality and quantity of sleep, which should not include long term use of over the counter sleep aids. Have your doctor review all of your medications to determine if certain medicines, or a mixture of, are putting you at a higher risk for Dementia.

Although there is no cure for most types of Dementia, including Alzheimer's, there are treatments that may slow progression. Medications are now being prescribed to temporarily improve symptoms as well as therapies to treat behavior problems caused by Dementia. Family members and caretakers of people suffering from Dementia play a critical role in supporting and applying remedies that aid in a better quality of life. There are numerous on-line and community support groups that can offer families free needed assistance.

Considering that approximately 12% of the American population (age 65 and older) suffers from some form of Dementia, it is critical that the conversation about risks, prevention, and treatment occur before it's too late (CDC, 2018). It is quite plausible that every American will have a family member suffer from Dementia. We live in a society that barely recognizes Psychological well-being as critical to our health care system. As a result, we must be diligent about arming ourselves with information, support, and the willingness to take action. Dementia is such a widespread and disruptive disease and deserves to be part of our healthy aging dialogue.

Chapter 9

The Anti-Aging Epidemic

In a society obsessed with youth, there are specific people and industries calling the shots as to how women should look and behave. And although women are fully engaged in the forever young ideology, it is primarily men who determine the standard. The male dominated industries that bombard us with images of attractive and desirable women have made it shameful for women to naturally age. In fact, billions of dollars are devoted to making women feel inadequate unless they commit to the products and procedures that will help them achieve a more youthful appearance.

Most women understand that the images they view on a daily basis via magazines, billboards, television, big screens, and social media are doctored and altered to achieve a very specific look. Further, women are well aware that even the young, thin, and beautiful models and actresses are physically transformed to portray a youthful, provocative appearance. But our knowledge of this unattainable image does not keep us from trying. Female public figures including actresses, journalists, politicians, and CEO's participate in the continual challenge to look young and attractive, just like they are supposed to. Female celebrities know that the way they look will be judged and scrutinized far more harshly than their male colleagues where age is often seen as sophisticated and distinguished. These women unfortunately understand that the peak of their career will most likely hit before they reach the ripe age of 30. In fact, according to a Time Magazine analysis of over 6,000 actors, men have their career peak at the age of 46, while female actors crown at age 30 (USA Today, Oliver, 2021). Further, opportunities for female roles reduce as women age and slightly increase for men. The audiences of the media expect a youthful and attractive woman on their screen and the industry owners they work for demand it.

Women in the public eye aren't the only ones contributing to the billion-dollar anti-aging industry. According to Globe News Wire (Market Research Company), the Anti-Aging Products Market in the United States is estimated at 14.2 billion dollars (2020) and continues to rise rapidly. The American Society of Plastic Surgeons claim that 16.7 billion dollars was spent on cosmetic procedures, alone, in the US in 2020 (yes- the year of the Pandemic when many optional procedures were cancelled). Many Cosmetic Surgeons reported that the large increase in patients was primarily due to the fact that people were viewing their faces up close, on screens, during the Pandemic. Too many people were discovering flaws that they hadn't noticed before. To clarify, "cosmetic" procedures and surgeries focus on a change in appearance, and "plastic" surgeries restore form and function. Plastic surgeries are not generally considered in the anti-aging statistics. To break these astronomical figures down into per person spending, could be a misleading number. So much of the research done is not specific as to the anti-aging products they are referring to. If the research is only referring to over the counter products then we would expect per person spending to be lower than the number that includes minimally invasive cosmetic procedures, such as Botox and fillers, as well as cosmetic surgeries that are so popular today. But for what it's worth, various research concludes that women spend approximately $250-$313 per month on anti-aging skincare and cosmetic products. Again, this number does not tell us if other anti-aging products (e.g. Vitamins, Rogaine, hair dye, sunscreen, etc.) were included in the studies. Ironically, according to a Consumer Reports Investigation (2006), anti-wrinkle creams don't make any substantial changes to aging skin. Even if the product user notices a difference, it will be slight and likely not to gain notice from others. This report also concluded that there is little to no correlation between the price of the product and its effectiveness.

Most studies suggest that the war on aging is increasingly raging. Minimally-invasive cosmetic procedures are gaining in popularity because results are more substantial than over the counter products and less expensive and invasive than surgeries. However, neurotoxins, dermal fillers, collagen stimulators, fat reduction, micro-needling, lasers, and chemical peels do not come cheap. For example, an average treatment of Botox simply to reduce the horizontal lines of the forehead runs about $250 and only lasts around 2-6 months. The average price for fillers to plump or raise the cheeks is approximately $1,000 and will need to be renewed after an estimated 12 months. More invasive solutions to aging are also gaining in popularity. Unfortunately, but not surprising, the breasts are the main culprit. In 2021, the top five surgical procedures included: Breast Augmentation (increase size), Abdominoplasty (tummy tuck), Mastopexy (breast lift), Breast Reduction, and Liposuction (Aesthetic Society, 2022).

While on the topic of products, I must make positive mention of the Dove Campaign for Real Beauty which has made efforts to broaden the definition of attractiveness. Dove challenged beauty stereotypes by selecting models whose appearances were outside the standard definitions of beautiful. These real and attractive women, albeit older, more wrinkled, and overweight, were more relatable and likeable to their female audience. The Dove Campaign gained a lot of attention and success for providing a more realistic standard for beauty. However, some feminist thought contends that the campaign is not all positive and question the motives and its relationship to other brands that contradict the Dove positive body image. I actually love the campaign and support its efforts in redefining the beautiful woman.

Clearly, the desire to look younger is not only psychologically distressing, but it comes at an impressive financial cost. Yet this information will most likely deter no one from buying the infinite amount of anti-aging products and procedures anyway; if even for the most insignificant differences. The bottom line is that women will attempt to look younger and more attractive at any cost. And those who can't afford it, are certainly at a greater disadvantage in the race for youth.

Our culture's obsession with youthful women is demonstrated in a 2018 study published in the journal *Science Advances* about online dating. This research studied the desirability of male and female users seeking opposite-sex partners. The main factor in determining desirability was based on the number of messages received by the nearly 200,000 users. The research determined that women found the men to be most desirable around the age of 50, and men found women to be most desirable at age 18. That's right! Men preferred women who were barely "of age".

Similar results were discovered in another study that looked at the data from the dating site OkCupid. This study found that men from the ages of 22-30 focused and preferred women younger than them. They also found that as men aged, they sought out younger and younger women, further widening the age gap between desirable mates. Developmental psychologists weighed in on the results of the online dating trends and concluded that perhaps evolutionary theories of mating should be considered, which suggests that men desire younger women because a youthful woman is generally a more fertile woman. Psychologists also suggested the theory that men are mostly interested in physical attractiveness and women are more attracted to a man with education and esteem (New York Times, Salam, 2018).

The avoidance of looking old has forged an endless effort of image editing. Every time I jump on Facebook, I struggle with viewing so many images of my female friends that have been significantly altered. There is a slew of tricks people use to simply pose for pictures that will enhance or hide their reality. I've learned that by simply bending forward slightly in a frontal photo, I can decrease the size of my legs and ass. If I look away from the lens and slightly downward, my eyelids don't look so drooped. If I use outdoor lighting, my sun spots and wrinkles aren't as prevalent. I haven't figured out why so many women use the selfie taken in the car in daylight, but I'm certain there is intent behind it. Truthfully, if I were more savvy about photoshop, I certainly would be tempted to take out wrinkles and frump, as well as add cheekbones and fullness to my hair. Instead, I am ridiculously choosy about what pictures I post.

When I see an altered selfie with the unrelated caption, I feel empathy towards the person posting, for I understand the validation she is hoping to get. I'm always struck by the reactionary comments about the altered selfie that gives the woman the exact words she was looking for: "You're beautiful." I can't decide if this is healthy or detrimental. I am on the fence as to whether or not these attempts at validating our looks is helping to boost confidence or simply manifesting the unrealistic definition of beauty that we should be shunning.

Summary

The resistance women have towards aging isn't simply a matter of fear; the fear of memory loss, physical decline, or even death. It is a more complex struggle that is provoked by a society that will strip her of value before reaching her potential. It is a fear that our appearance will not meet the standard of our cultures' definition of desirable. What a tragic message we feed our daughters. It is time that we reject these expressions and challenge the perceptions of attractiveness, sensuality, and success.

I dream of a day when an army of wrinkled skin and silver haired women will stand up to the unrealistic expectations of beauty and define for the world what it really looks like to be prized. But it will take an enormous army to put the youth-pushing product industries out of business. It will take a sizable infantry to change social media and film to include positive representations of older women. Ironically, we will need a monumental legion of women to convince each other that we can age in the way we were meant to. But until this army is assembled, I will personally change my mindset and embrace my gorgeous wrinkles, my experienced body, and my whimsical mind; all that make me the "imperfect" woman I was meant be.

Part Three – Their Story

There is no more powerful tool for graceful aging than to adhere to the wisdom of those who have found peace with their final descent.

~ Michelle Player

Chapter 10

The Art of Joyful Aging

When I first established residency in the mountains of Colorado, I felt as though I had arrived at a beautiful vacation destination. For the next several months, I behaved as a tourist, experiencing the rivers, lakes, trails, boutiques, and restaurants. Life without a job was fantastic... well mostly. At some point, I knew I had to contribute to the family wallet and establish a responsible daily routine. Mostly, I was hoping to stumble upon my new purpose.

As the Colorado summer was replaced with fall foliage and cooler temperatures, I knew my outdoor adventures would temporarily pause. I am not a winter enthusiast. I do not like to ski and I only pretend to enjoy sledding to appease my family who are more temperature tolerant and less fearful of heights. At that point in time, I had yet to find employment that suited my wants and needs. I knew boredom was about to set in.

Meanwhile, my daughter, Amelia, started school as a 10th grader. Cruelly, this kid has to find her place in a new school where clicks were pre-established and every kid looked the same (those are Amelia's words). Amelia understood the value of diversity and was a little taken aback by the lack of. My husband and I had to laugh at this observation because for her entire life, we lived in a suburb of Salt Lake City where white and Mormon culture overwhelmingly dominated. Nonetheless, she may have needed yet another excuse to be unhappy about our move. I couldn't blame her.

As I drove Amelia to and from school daily, we passed by a large, adobe, pink building that was home to several elderly residents. This Assisted Living Center was also home to many deer who often grazed on the front lawn, seemingly unaware of their human audience.

One day, while driving by, I asked Amelia if she was interested in volunteering at this center. I explained that her involvement would occupy some of her free time and allow her a sense of purpose. She agreed.

The offer of her services was met with unintended results. Evidently, volunteer help was needed mostly during day time hours in a residency where dinner was served at 4:30; a time when most of us are just thinking about what to withdraw from the freezer. 'After dinner hours' in an Assisted Living Center are mostly spent in the quiet comfort of their individual rooms, hoping not to be disturbed. Therefore, only I, and not Amelia, had the daytime availability to be a regular volunteer.

In all honesty, I had no experience or desire to work with the elderly. I had spent the last 35 years working with children, who let me be in charge and rarely judged me. I wasn't sure if I was cut out for this position. After all, I feared old people smells, petrified finger and toe nails, and strong opinions (the confidence in not giving a damn). But I signed up. I couldn't look at my daughter and say, "Not for me." Besides, surrounding myself with the elderly population seemed like an opportunity to be educated on the sociology of aging.

What started out as a two hour per week commitment, quickly morphed into about fifteen hours per week of time spent with a very old population. Not only was I finding these people interesting and entertaining, but I was being mentored by a woman who stroked my ego by declaring that I was a Super Star Volunteer. This woman whom, for the sake of her privacy, I will call Caffeine, after the energy source I need daily. At 71 years of age, Caffeine had more energy and initiative than anyone I had met. Ironically though, she did not consume any drinks containing caffeine. It's true, no coffee or soda for this warrior.

Somehow, my role at the center became that of "Arts & Crafts Instructor" and "Bulletin Board Designer." I was also in charge of the property greenhouse which would eventually house several flowers and vegetables outsourced for their kitchen and gardens. While these tasks allowed me to dig in the dirt and re-live the best of my creative elementary school years, I found myself more drawn to simply spending time chatting with the residents. I quickly discovered that they all had a story worth telling.

I would love to honor all my new friends by sharing their stories. But I will focus on the experiences that have had the most profound impact on my view of aging. I have no doubt that it is the "stories" that affect us most. There

is no more powerful tool for graceful aging than to adhere to the wisdom of those who have found peace with their final descent.

Introducing Lucy

Lucy, age 82 ish, is a tall, slender woman who loves to wear jeans and bright lipstick. She is one of the more active residents, always walking and socializing. Her roommate is her beloved dog, Charlie. The first time I met Lucy, was at Doughnut Social, where she was drinking coffee out of a brown mug belonging to the residency. After introductions to one another, Lucy said to me, "Don't you think that this place should have more colorful mugs?" Stunned by her odd but very reasonable question, she continued before I could answer. "Brown is blah and we need less blah in our lives." I agreed. Now this woman had caught my interest. I needed an invite into her room. I tried several times to visit Lucy, but could not seem to catch her home. One day, however, in passing her room, the cleaning staff had the door propped open. Inside her room was the most incredible display of color. I walked in, alerting the cleaning staff that I was looking for Lucy. I was told that she was out walking Charlie. There was no way in hell I could exit this wonderland without further observation. Every nook and cranny was occupied by some fascinating item. This floor to ceiling display of beautiful materials, vibrant flowers, brightly painted furniture, polished red appliances, stunning art on the walls, colorful rubber balls, a floor piano mat, and other unique décor flooded the small room like a kaleidoscope. But somehow, it worked. The room looked like it was home to an optimistic and spunky artist. I instantly realized why Lucy hated our brown coffee mugs.

In the weeks following Lucy's move to the facility, I noticed a change to the outdoor landscape. In the colorless days of winter, Lucy had managed to brighten up the courtyard, visible from the street. Lucy had strategically placed colorful silk flowers in the trees that she viewed from her window. She also had several vibrant colored pots, dripping with plastic flowers and ornaments. Several metal garden decorations were randomly placed in the grass. The three-foot-tall metal giraffe, sporting the American flag and moved around weekly, was my favorite yard decoration. She had made her own outdoor seating area with two red chairs as well as a bright lime green, three-piece patio set, always with balloons or gadgets attached. Lucy had balloons delivered to the center about once a month, simply to brighten the place up.

Lucy had a huge heart and tended to fuss and worry about all the residents. She took the time to get to know her neighbors and found goodness in everyone. I loved that Lucy became somewhat of a cheerleader for her friends. When a resident walked into a common area, Lucy would announce them and share something positive about the person. I must admit that getting the "Lucy Introduction" made me feel loved and a bit famous. Lucy also took the time to acknowledge and appreciate life's little pleasures. She would comment on the beauty of the potted flowers and express her satisfaction with the newly installed shade sails. She was the first to notice holiday decorations and the best at spotting even the most minor residential repairs. Lucy loved music and would often find herself in a transfixed groove as the pulse of the tunes blasted from the residential boom box.

I'm always trying to spend time with Lucy but she is rarely still. Lucy has so much to explore and learn on a daily basis. Her curiosity and desire for a daily thrill leaves me envious. How inspiring to see a woman of her age still soaking in the wonders and colors of life. I have a feeling that Lucy carries some brilliant secrets about happiness and aging that I hope to uncover. For now, I will watch Lucy live in the moment and simply appreciate her rainbow.

Meet Dixie

Dixie had just celebrated her 95th Birthday. Her and I have had a connection since day one. On my first day as a volunteer, I was walking a group of women down the hall with armfuls of Halloween decorations, when Dixie began to teeter. She reached for the table and called out that she thought she may be having a heart attack. I quickly grabbed on to Dixie and eased her into a chair. Dixie's breathing became more labored and she started profusely sweating. I began to feel like I was under water without the ability to hear, see, or even breath. The other residents quickly surrounded Dixie and began to stroke her hair, kiss her cheeks, and talk her through the crisis. I knew I had to snap out of my own underwater retreat and do something quick. I was able to yell down the hall for help and separate her from the terrified and swarming women. Dixie was taken by ambulance to the hospital.

I returned the next day to learn that Dixie was fine. She had a pacemaker that will sometimes cause the reaction I witnessed. I told Dixie that she gave me the finest initiation a girl could ever get for a first day on the job. She said, "You're welcome," and we became friends.

Dixie was eventually put on hospice because of her incurable cancer. She knew that she was dying. If facing this heartache wasn't sad enough, her daughter who lived in another state was also dying of cancer. Dixie yearned to be with her daughter but was not strong enough to withstand the travel, nor was her daughter. So, they comforted each other at a distance. I had known Dixie for several months before I was made aware of her situation. I always assumed that Dixie was quite healthy because of her positive attitude and regular attendance at all of the social activities. Her favorite activity, lucky for me, was Arts and Crafts. It always surprised Dixie when her projects turned out well. She giggled and proclaimed, "I didn't know that I could do that."

One day Dixie asked me if I wouldn't mind teaching her how to paint on canvas. I asked what she wanted to paint and she said, "Anything." I explained that I was an Arts & Crafts impersonator and that I had no talent at painting. She said, "That's a shame because I've always wanted to learn how to do that." My heart sank and after a few minutes of thought, I told Dixie that I would bring in Amelia, my daughter, to teach her how to paint. Thankfully, Amelia is a true artist and has studied painting techniques.

In preparation for Amelia's lesson, Dixie had me order an easel, paints and brushes. She wanted this artistic experience to be official. Amelia and I came in and set up the make-shift art studio in Dixie's very warm room. After convincing Dixie that she could make mistakes and paint over them, she relaxed and began to follow the directions Amelia was giving her. With a shaky and arthritic hand, Dixie was able to paint a pine tree; Amelia's, straight and stout while Dixie's was crooked and whimsical. She proudly named her painting, "Pine Tree in the Wind". She proclaimed, "I'm looking forward to the next lesson."

I could not figure out why Dixie would want to learn how to paint considering her difficult circumstances. She had minimal eyesight. Her left hand had limited movement and as mentioned… she was dying. Why would she want to invest time and energy into learning a new task? What kept her curious and still interested, knowing that her days were numbered? I did not have the nerve to ask Dixie these questions, but I think I know what she may have said... "Why not?" Then she would giggle.

Two weeks after Dixie painted "Tree in the Wind" she laid in her bed fighting for every breath. I took a private moment to let her know how grateful I was to have been her friend and that I would plant a crooked pine tree in my yard to serve as a reminder to keep learning as she had. Dixie passed away as dignified as she lived.

Here's Gene

Gene was 81ish years of age, yet looked much younger. She maintained a slim physique and dressed in a very updated fashion. Red framed glasses and bright orange slip-on shoes were her fashion staple. Unfortunately, Gene suffered from the cruelest disease; Alzheimer's. Some of the time, Gene was aware of her failing memory and would apologize for not being able to answer questions. But most the time, Gene seemed unaware that our conversation had repeated multiple times in the same sitting. I was incredibly drawn to Gene because of her aura. When I walked into a room full of residents, it was easy to spot Gene, waltzing through the crowd, smiling and conversing with a slight southern accent and with the confidence of a celebrity. She truly sparkled.

I had the opportunity to enter Gene's domain in order to help her phone her daughters. She was missing them and simply wanted to touch base. When I entered Gene's room, I instantly noticed that her room was well-kept and classy. It also smelled of fresh linen, which was coming from an incense vaporizer. Of course, I immediately began scanning the numerous photos decorating the walls and shelves. Her family was stunningly gorgeous and it was clear to me that Gene had always been the Belle of the Ball.

Not only did I learn that Gene was an English teacher, but she was also an artist. She talked lovingly about her students and how much she missed them. Gene's most prized possession, besides her daughters, was a bust of her late husband. Gene actually sculpted it herself and it was exquisite. Gene talked frequently about their love and teared up over his absence. Unfortunately, I have listened to her painful story of loss numerous times because Gene forgets that she has already shared it with me. In fact, Gene asked me who I was several times a day. She knows my face well and started referring to me as "Sister", a title I'm honored to bear. When Gene saw me, she would immediately approach me with a hug and say, "What are we going to do now, Sister?"

One day, Gene and I were hanging out in her room when she suddenly became distracted by the bust. She began to run her fingers carefully over the face, expressing in a whisper, how perfectly she remembered Tom's eyes, nose, mouth, and even mustache. As if Tom were listening, she murmured, "You were perfect." I didn't want to interrupt this moment and attempted to slip out the door without being noticed. Besides, I was tearing up and I didn't want Gene to see me. But when I reached the door, she snapped out of her memory and turned to me and asked, "So what are we going to do now, Sister?"

I struggled with having observed this moment. Gene's mind was no longer able to hold short term information, but she still held to memories from long ago – sometimes. Yesterday, Gene didn't know that her husband had passed, but today, she ached, knowing that he was a memory.

So, what keeps Gene motivated? Is it robotics; doing what she has always done because it is automatic? Is it her personality or nature that keeps her happily bustling? Or is it a choice to live her best life? I suspect that it is a combination of the three.

My girl, Gene, has been descending from her summit for some time now. She has moved into the Memory Care unit and struggles to put words together to form a sentence. When I visit, she holds tightly to my hand and wants me to walk with her. She still enjoys music and will break out into dance when the right rhythm triggers her memory. Once while we were doing "Buffalos" down the hallway (a tap step that we are both familiar with), I asked Gene, "What keeps you so happy all the time, Sister?" She responded with a huge smile, "What else ya gonna do?"

- -

Never did I think that an Assisted Living Center would be a place where I would find some solace in death. I anticipated that my fears of aging and dying would be triggered and validated on a daily basis. On the contrary, my elderly friends have shown me, unintentionally, how to gracefully and courageously descend from the mountain top. They have exemplified perseverance, curiosity, and the art of staying positive. My elderly friends have demonstrated how significant and gratifying the last section of the trail can be. Their final miles do not come without stumbles and grief and not everyone's trail is equally accommodating. But my elderly friends have made me hopeful that my own path can be interesting, colorful, and even joyous.

Chapter 11

The Secret Uncovered

The negative diet we are continually fed in our culture profoundly dictates our view of aging. Most people struggle both physically and psychologically with the challenges of growing old and seek the magic key to aging with grace. We have yet to read the headline that proclaims that the aging secrets have been discovered and that we will all have access to this sacred information. So, like many youth seekers, I too, joined the treasure hunt, looking for the magic formula. What I am about to share with you is groundbreaking. According to the comprehensive research, *the key to healthy & happy aging exists!* This is not the moment to bookmark the page and continue reading later. You are about to learn how to age! You're welcome.

As a youngster, I remember watching NBC's "Today" show with Willard Scott. Willard would announce the birthday celebrations of several people in the United States who were turning 100. I was fascinated by this achievement because making it to the century mark was inconceivable in my young mind. I paid close attention to the advice of each centenarian as they explained their secrets to living so long. Many would claim that simple activities like a daily glass of gin, naps, having a pet, singing opera in the shower, playing poker, and other random past times held the secret to longevity. I took mental note, of course.

I have since learned that Willard Scott was not actually revealing the true secrets of aging well. Yet what I did not realize at the time was there existed a common thread between these centenarians as they shared encouraging and humorous answers. The mystery behind happy and healthy aging simply boiled down to OPTIMISM.

I repeat, the key to aging well is Optimism!

No shit? That is the secret ingredient? Years of collective research on the aging population conclude that the number one factor in health, happiness, and longevity is a person's optimism. Go ahead and scoff at this conclusion. Feel a bit disappointed. I did! I expected a more scientific explanation. I wanted a pill that would fix my aging concerns. I can swallow a pill, no problem. But being an optimist? This feels like the time you hunted the house for your glasses, only to realize they were sitting on top of your head the entire time! Optimism sounds too simple, yet its' application sounds incredibly hard – for most. But the fact remains; the outcome of the aging battle will highly depend on a positive mindset. Damn it.

Some people are naturally optimistic. If you are not one of those people, there are ways to improve your optimism:

- **Reframe Situations**
  Maintaining perspective by seeing the difficult situation in its entirety rather than focusing on the negative components. Think of the challenges as opportunities. Learn from the situation.

- **Set Goals**
  Set daily achievable goals. Be specific and realistic with your goals then have the confidence to achieve them.
- **Have Gratitude**
  Set aside time every day to remind yourself of all that you are grateful for and proud of.
- **Strengthen Relationships**
  Optimism is related to strong social networks. Spend time with friends and family. Avoid being alone for long periods of time. Surround yourself with supportive and positive people.
- **Practice Random Acts of Kindness**
  People who volunteer or perform kind acts for others tend to be happier people. Practicing kind acts is just as rewarding as receiving them.
- **Find Purpose**
  Everyone needs to feel like they are contributing to society. Find ways to matter. Volunteer, help friends and neighbors, reach out to others, own a pet, properly maintain house and yard, teach...

My time at the Assisted Living Center has given me a fresh lens in which to view the aging process. My goal was to understand why growing old affected people so differently. Selfishly, I wanted to discover the mindset of people who seemed to get along well with their aging self so that I could mimic their practices. I needed to know if an optimistic mindset was really the main factor in quality aging.

One day I had a conversation with Caffeine (Activities Director) regarding her opinion on healthy aging. Her and

I witnessed daily the routines and personalities of several elderly people and often made comparisons. I inquired about the happiest and healthiest residents versus the "unicorns" and wanted to know her conclusion as to the "how" and "why" the differences. Caffeine summated that she believed the difference between happy and miserable aging could primarily be determined by the choice an individual makes about "living in the moment – or not". Her conclusion sounded simple and a bit cliché' at the time, but would eventually make a lot of sense to me.

To summarize, I discovered that my friends at the Assisted Living Center fit into one of three categories. The first category, I labeled "Earthly Purgatory." The Second group I referred to as "Expired," The last category I called "Present."

Earthly Purgatory

Purgatory is a state of eternal punishment and damnation. From a religious view, Purgatory would be the place one gets "stuck"; neither heaven nor hell. From an aging perspective, people who live in Earthly Purgatory are tortured by their inability to continue living the "good ol' days." Many people choose to remain so attached to what *used* to be that they struggle accepting the reality of what is. Some of my friends at the facility seem to obsess on what their life no longer offers them. Further, the Earthly Purgatory Group continue to grieve the loss of their youth as well as loved ones. It seems as though the grieving process is relentless, almost torturous. This mindset evokes anger, frustration, and restlessness. I observed that these people want to voice their troubles on a regular basis. It seems important to them that everyone know about their more relevant past; when they were lively and valuable. This group has ultimately lost who they are. They haven't discovered ways to adapt to their reluctant bodies and forgetful minds.

If I were to ask someone of the Earthly Purgatory mindset if they were looking forward to the holidays, I would likely get a response similar to this: "There was a time that I enjoyed Christmas, surrounded by all the kids and grandkids. But I never see them anymore because they all have their own lives to worry about. So, I'm not that thrilled to be spending Christmas with the few people who may remember that I'm still around."

Expired

This group of people literally live like the title I discreetly assigned them, Expired. These people have one foot in the grave. The Expired can only see their future, which appears to be bleak and coming to an end at any moment. They dwell on their aches and pains and often have multiple medical issues that may be exasperated by their attitude on life. The Expired tend to socially isolate themselves and often suffer from depression. They are not interested nor see a point in participating in activities or learning anything new. Sadly, this group has lost their grit and fight. It is difficult to offer assistance to them because they are not interested in committing to the work it would take to improve their situation. Essentially, they have given up.

If I were to ask someone of the Expired mindset if they were looking forward to the holidays, I would likely get a response similar to this: "I may not make it to Christmas and if I do, it will feel like any other day of the year. When you're this old and broken, there isn't much to look forward to anymore."

Present

This category of people, who live in the moment, are certainly the ones who seem the healthiest and happiest. The Present people appreciate what has been lived and what is left to live, all while mindful of what can be gained from any one moment in time. The common motto I hear with this group is, "I just take life one day at a time." Of course, they mourn the loss of their past but it is NOT their focus. Of course, they know that their time is limited, but they choose to NOT dwell on that either. These people appreciate their gifts and occupy their minds with busy daily routines and new activities. These people keep a distance from the crabs and surround themselves with like-minded and positive individuals. Not everyone in this category have a clean bill of health. In fact, many suffer from chronic and debilitating illnesses like Cancer, Dementia, Arthritis, etc. Yet their optimistic mindset serves as their medication to a more active and fulfilling life.

If I were to ask someone of the Present mindset if they were looking forward to the holidays, I would likely get a response similar to this: "Yes! I hope we get snow! What are your holiday plans?"

The recipe to happy aging is not surprising nor unfamiliar. The ingredients are actually more common knowledge than we care to admit and can be applied to any stage of life. Perhaps one of the biggest obstacles is the fact that being happy is a *mindset* and being healthy is *difficult work*. Further, as we age we lose the energy, willpower, and social support to continue the investment. It feels more sensible and worth it to invest in our younger selves.

There are factors in healthy aging that are simply out of our control, some of which include, genetics, socioeconomics, access to health care, air quality, education, and work/home environment. While it is unfortunate that we are unable to manage many determinants of happy aging, we do have some control over other critical factors including, diet, exercise, social engagements, spirituality, and mindset.

I don't consider myself an optimist, but I am not a pessimist either. I am a Libra. Libras are supposedly well-balanced and our Zodiac sign is a scale to signify that harmony. In fact, I have a tattoo of a set of scales on the back of my neck to serve as a brag badge of balance. I expose this part of me because I have come to live by a motto of balance. I fully accept that there is a constant exchange of forces that must occur in order to create harmony in life. We must know darkness to see the light. We must know bad to appreciate good. We must experience sad to understand happy. We must go through difficult times to value more comfortable times. To embrace this life as a balancing act helps me to realize that my pain will pass when the scales return to their symmetrical state.

It's difficult to be an optimist, I know. Yet, I challenge myself daily to find the silver linings. I also remind myself that I have a choice in how I perceive my situation. I don't want to be in Earthly Purgatory where my playlist only includes songs from my past. Nor do I want to be Expired where having a playlist doesn't even matter. I want to be Present where I can enjoy a playlist of assorted rhythms, both old and new, in which others will want to join me in song and dance.

Chapter 12

The Plague of 2020

Initially, there was a small amount of buzz on the news about a virus in China that had the potential of spreading quickly and killing many. Like several news reports, it seemed distant from my life and therefore, I didn't give it much concern. What suddenly caught my attention, however, was the headline about the virus entering an Assisted Living Center in Washington State and taking multiple lives without warning. This hit close to home, especially considering that I was working in a similar fragile environment.

The pandemic of 2020 snuck into our lives and paralyzed the world in a matter of weeks. Like most, I suffered from a strange emotional turbulence. Living in a state of fear on a daily basis resulted in an inconceivable personal crisis. Being confined to my home made me feel both lethargic and restless. Having to social distance myself from all human contact was completely unnatural.

My house arrest team which included me, my husband, daughter, and dog did our best to stay active and positive. My spouse set up his office space in the living room. My daughter had her school base camp just ten feet away from his; technically in the kitchen. My home office was the bedroom, which proved to be an unproductive and gloomy choice. We all grew tired and annoyed with each other as we unintentionally invaded one another's space. My daughter did not appreciate my tasteless lounge outfits and untidy hair as I waltzed past her classmates on Zoom simply to get myself a snack. My husband grew agitated at my constant interruptions, as I accidently spoke to the only two humans I could have face-to-face interaction with. The two-square court was set up in the garage where we would often break for tension release. We frequented the mountain trails in order to escape the house, but discovered that everyone had the same idea.

Just weeks into the nightmare, I missed my daily routine and was growing more anxious as cabin fever set in. I would tie a bandana to my face and nervously venture out into public places. To view other people in similar attire and with the same hesitant gate made me feel as though we were all shell-shocked, crawling out from shelters, curious about the damage. The streets were empty and most businesses closed. Guarded with face coverings and hand sanitizer, people purposefully walked at a distance from each other. The awkwardness spurred an apologetic glance, maybe a nod, at one another. Seeing bare shelves in the stores caused me to have small panic attacks that I disguised out of embarrassment. Who knew that toilet paper would be such a hot commodity? My dad had to mail us a package of toilet paper when we were down to our last roll. We had thought of numerous options for wiping, but all involved a degree of weirdness. Luckily the package arrived with just a few squares to spare. Dinners were interesting as choices were limited. The produce section didn't take the same hit as storable food. One night I served game hen and salad. It tasted fine but I really craved a rotisserie chicken.

I found myself terrified every time I watched the news, but I couldn't turn it off. Like many, I needed an escape. My numbing choice was alcohol. Liquor took the edge off and my spouse and I became too friendly with this line of defense. We eventually weaned ourselves off of the excessive use, but it took a while. I found it odd, though I didn't complain, that the liquor store remained open out of "necessity" yet the library, gym, schools, and most businesses closed their doors. What a strange time.

My daughter had been training for her 4th Degree Black Belt in Mixed Martial Arts (indeed, she is a bad ass). She was supposed to travel to San Francisco to test for her belt, but all was halted due to Covid. Instead, Amelia had to train from home and perform her skills in front of the all too familiar computer screen. We turned our rental home into a make-shift Martial Arts' studio as couches and tables went into the garage and all breakables were tucked away. My husband and I had to step into the ring when partnering skills were being demonstrated. We did our best to learn the skill well enough to allow her to fully demonstrate, but we were clearly not in Black Belt shape. She tested from the living room in Colorado that June of 2020 and proudly received her Mastery Level Belt (4th degree Black Belt). This experience proved to be one of the silver linings interwoven throughout such a difficult time.

The Assisted Living Center where I was working part-time diligently followed pandemic guidelines. The fragility of this environment resulted in a significant interruption of daily life. No longer could families come into the facility to visit loved ones. Whoever made this rule may not have appreciated all the necessary caregiving that most families provide to their loved ones, like "open wound care" (rashes, bed sores, skin irritations, etc.), trimming nails, cutting and dying hair, shaving, massaging, brushing teeth and dentures, deep cleaning rooms, entertaining, assistance with mail and paperwork, organizing, and other daily responsibilities. The care staff, in an instant, became nurses, estheticians, beauticians, therapists, custodians, personal assistants, waiters, sanitizers, entertainers, and wardens.

All activities ceased. All couches were removed and replaced by chairs, 6 feet apart. The dining hall continually closed when even one person had been exposed to Covid. When the dining hall was open, every meal was divided into three groups in order to reduce the amount of people in one room. This made for lengthy meal times where staff had to oversee rotations and service, while simultaneously performing other duties. All outside volunteers and entertainment was halted. Residents were encouraged to stay in their rooms with the exception of walking the halls for minimal exercise. Residents could not leave the facility except for an approved doctor's appointment.

All staff and residents were masked. I always questioned the rationale behind masking the residents. These people lived together. They shared the same common areas including activity rooms, communal bathrooms, dining hall, mail rooms, hallways, courtyards, and the like. On the outside of the residency, families formed cohorts or pods of people that did not have to mask or socially distance from each other. For some unexplained reason, the residents did not get this luxury. According to CDC Guidelines, they were expected to conduct their lives as though everyone they lived with put them at great risk. Further, many residents, especially those suffering from Dementia, did not understand the unnatural rules, therefore, keeping them masked and socially distanced was nearly impossible.

Families grew worried about the mental and physical state of their loved ones. Communication between a resident and his/her family became the responsibility of the staff. Many were using their personal cell phones to call or FaceTime resident's families. It was heart wrenching to watch families stand outside of windows in an attempt visit. Most residents are hard of hearing and have poor eyesight, making the window visits quite frustrating for all involved. Eventually, outdoor, socially distanced, masked visits were allowed, but had to be monitored by a staff member to ensure that no one was unmasked or receiving much needed hugs.

The pandemic raged on; easing up only to then mutate and send the world in reverse. Guidelines were constantly changing. Of course, confusion and conflict among our leaders and health organizations made matters worse. People, it seemed, were in a dryer, tumbling on a high cycle and desperately clinging to the hope that this will all end. Yet when the dryer momentarily stopped, the separation of people was evident. Like our laundry, we had been sorted and separated. Masks, vaccines, guidelines; all washed with politics. A time of crisis so absurdly becomes one of our most divisive moments in history.

The frailty of our society accelerated as the death of George Floyd scarred our nation. Already glued to our screens, hideous images of Cultural and Institutional racism shed light on a perpetual ugliness of our society. The Black Lives Matter movement ignited change and racial justice but was sadly met with resistance. Protests of racial discrimination briefly took the stage of our divided country, but had to compete with an ongoing pandemic and approaching political elections. So much was at stake for our country and for our individual mental health.

The fragility of our nation was paralleled with the circumstances inside the homes and facilities of the elderly. Although the virus did not seem to discriminate, the older population suffered the gravest consequences. According to PBS News, by December of 2021, 75% of all Covid deaths were of people age 65 and older. The New York Times reported that 1 of every 100 older Americans (65+) had perished due to Covid. These statistics drove the guidelines that put our elders in extreme fear and isolation. Many lives were likely saved by the strict regulations but not without enormous psychological and economic damage.

In an industry that already suffered from low wages and high turnover, the Pandemic created another crisis for employees of Assisted Care. As mentioned, the responsibilities of each care-giver dramatically increased. While attempting to wear many hats, care-givers had to manage their own fears about Covid while calming the nerves of those they cared for as well as residents' families. The thought of possibly bringing Covid into this fragile work environment was incredibly stressful for care-givers.

In the beginning of the Pandemic, I was assisting with activities on a part-time basis. But about two weeks into the crisis, my life was thrown into a tailspin when the Executive Administrator made a personal decision to leave, with only a couple of days' notice. In a desperate attempt to keep the facility afloat until the proper replacement could be found, I was asked to step into a leadership role. Holy Shit. As flattered as I was, I knew that I was not the right person to run an Assisted Living Center. I had not a clue as to how to manage such a facility, but I did have the heart (so I was told).

In just the first week of my new position, the learning curve was pitched to me at about 100 mph. I spent long days attempting to learn the complex particulars of care-giving facilities. I discovered that "Care Giving" involved multiple regulations and practices that needed constant monitoring and training.

I received a crash course regarding state regulations and avoidance of citations. I familiarized myself with the laws concerning patient rights and the various advocacy groups to support the residents. I also had to learn of the various resources available to families for a variety of elderly issues, including Memory Care programs and support groups. I discovered that administering medications to residents required training and licensing and that mistakes in distribution could be fatal. I came to understand that communication with pharmacies and primary care-givers had to occur regularly, clearly, and through the proper channels. I quickly learned that HIPPA (the protection of health records and information) was taken incredibly seriously and that the mere mention of someone's circumstance could violate their privacy. I became familiar with policies regarding food service and development of well-balanced menus. I discovered that the numerous allergies to food and other elements needed constant consideration. I learned the differences between private insurances, Medicare, and Medicaid as well as the bureaucracy of implementing any of them. I was made aware of the importance of constant communication with families and that they did not want explanations, but wanted resolutions. I unfortunately had to learn that people will physically and psychologically decline after being isolated for lengthy periods of time. I discovered that preparing work schedules was a nightmare, considering low staff numbers and the fact that if someone called in sick, was late, or simply quit, there was no option to do without an employee; the residents needed assistance. I learned that managing employees who worked for minimum wage was challenging, considering that many of them had additional jobs, school, and/or family obligations. I discovered that people resent you for a quick climb up the ladder. I learned that being a leader in an Assisted Living Center in the middle of a fucking pandemic was about the worst place I could imagine myself in.

I committed to giving myself to the facility for 90 days. I could not devote indefinitely considering my lack of training and unwillingness to invest in the required education to properly serve the role I was given. Further, I knew that the Pandemic would loom over this environment and that if Covid entered our doors under my leadership, I would have to oversee a potentially very distressful and sad affair. Nonetheless, the 90-day experience proved to be one that I will never regret. For all the stress and frustrations I endured, I learned so many valuable lessons about an essential industry serving a treasured population. My most rewarding lesson, however, was that of bravery.

Even prior to the Pandemic, I recognized the stoicism of the elderly residents. Knowing that their finish line is near must certainly require a daily dose of courage. Most residents did not speak about a fear of death. Several residents welcomed their passing from a spiritual mindset and some merely wanted their pain to cease. Most residents simply found ways to accept the inevitable, realizing that they have no control over this fate. It became apparent to me that my friends, with age, had developed resiliency and courage to face any challenge put before them. Their bravery was never about an absence of fear, but the courage to carry on in spite of fear.

My friends have grown familiar with what I like to call the Art of Living, which embraces the idea that the world continues to revolve with or without our permission. So, when the Pandemic hit, I wasn't surprised by the bravery the residents continued to reveal. This older population, although well aware of the fact that they were at high risk for Covid complications and death, remained calm and logical. While staff and families nervously grappled with our new reality, the residents seemed to take it in stride. There was certainly fear of the unknown and the possible loss of lives, but again, let us not confuse fear with bravery. What could have been pure pandemonium, was instead met with composure and courage.

Several months after my departure, I learned that Covid had entered the facility we strived so hard to protect. Sadly, lives were lost. The following year, after having time to reflect, I came back to the facility to teach movement classes to the residents I adored. While I teach them about the mechanics and benefits of moving, they continue to teach me about the power of living courageously. I hope through their influence and example that I am better prepared to face the numerous obstacles that life will present. I have no doubt that the Pandemic of 2020 was one of the ultimate tests of courage that will forever remind the world of both our strength and fragility.

Part Four – End of Story

"My mother always used to say, 'The older you get, the better you get, unless you're a banana'."

~ Betty White

Chapter 13

Aging Oddly or Oddly Aging?

In full disclosure, I am a little hesitant to include the topic regarding old people and their odd ways. But we all see it; in our parents, older neighbors and friends, and even in ourselves! I can't ignore it. Perhaps this subject matter will perpetuate the negative stereotypes of the elderly that I wish to rid, or, I'm hoping, that an honest dialogue will reveal that strange behavior in the elderly may not be so unusual after all.

Repetitious stories

By far, the topic that comes up most about my parents when my siblings and I are swapping gossip, is the fact that they get stuck on the same handful of stories that we've heard a million times. You know, those stories that when the conversation goes there, you immediately tune out. Some of the stories are wonderful and worthy of repetition, to a point. Then there are the repeated narratives that almost anger you because they are so controversial, or worse, boring! The clever conversationalists have discovered ways to navigate around their dreaded recaps. But many of us find ourselves trapped in the narrative we could recite in our sleep. What is this about?

The obvious answer is that many elderly people repeat their stories because they simply forget that they have already told them. Whether this is due to the natural decline of cognitive function or some level of Dementia, memory lapse can be the reason for repetitious stories. Unfortunately, this defense doesn't help the audience enjoy the tale for the 49th time.

But there are other reasons that older people beat their stories to death that may not be considered when you are taking offense or zoning out in conversations.

Many elderly people are retired and living a fairly solitary and simplified lifestyle. They find themselves doing mundane tasks that are routine, even habitual. The big event for the week may be going to the doctor's office. When you take yourself out of traffic, public places, work environments, and social events, life can be, well... boring. If nothing new is happening, then you will resort to the story lines that own some level of excitement. If they don't resort to their more exciting "go-to stories", then you will most likely talk about weather, health conditions, television programs, and next-door neighbors.

Older people repeat their stories out of a desire to remind their audience that there was a time when their life was more stimulating and they were more visible. Some refer to the past as the "good ol' days" and some talk as though it were the "worst of times." Either way, the nostalgic story line is an avenue for them to reminisce about a time they felt more included and important in this world. Their story may be a reminder not to view them in a manner in which we often view our "old" belongings: dated, useless, and time to toss out or turn over to charity. Unlike younger generations, the elderly (for now) primarily leave their legacy through verbal and written communication. Being known or remembered is captured through storytelling, journals, and letters. Whereas younger generations have the means to extensively document their life through advancing technology and media and share it on a daily basis. Therefore, in the latter stage of life, it becomes more significant to verbally repeat the stories that will validate their existence.

Well known behaviorist, Erik Erikson (1959), who determined that personality develops in a predetermined order known as the Eight Stages of Psychosocial Development, suggested that in order to achieve "Ego Integrity instead of Despair" (stage 8), older adults have a need to review their experiences to create a coherent sense of self (Cherry, 2021). In other words, it is beneficial for older people to reminisce in order to establish a comprehensive understanding of their life. In fact, reminiscing, or life in review, is often used in therapy to treat the elderly for depression. Many therapists would agree that there exists a human need to reflect on the past and consider all the experiences that have shaped who we are and the legacy we will leave behind. By sharing these thoughts, the elderly are attempting to find meaning from their circumstances and choices in life.

So, when you find yourself annoyed with a loved one who continually repeats their life stories, take a deep breath and try to find the patience to listen, for the experienced lifers are inherently organizing their thoughts and may provide you with helpful advice and wisdom.

Time Warp

As a kid, I loved going to my grandparents' house where I could count on consistency in just about everything. From a toddler to an adult, the same toys, furniture, décor, food, cars, clothing, and hairstyles, would be a familiar comfort at grandma's house. Every holiday came with the same decorations that have somehow lasted through the decades. Their dated cars were kept clean without remnants of busy lifestyles tossed about the seats. Not much ever changed and I liked it. But now, as I struggle to keep up with the Jones' and continually adapt my style to stay current and hip, I wonder when my day will come when I don't give a damn about being current and fashionable. I can't decide if I admire or fault their time warp. I'm not even sure if this is a topic that leaves anyone else curious and fascinated. But I wanted to tackle it. I wanted to explore the reasons for the elderly to find themselves stalled in time.

The stuck in time observation comes with little research to back it up. I find this peculiar because most, but not all, of the elderly people in *my* life exhibit the "stuck in time" phenomenon and it is frequently depicted in media. One of my favorite examples is characterized in the sitcom *Everybody Loves Raymond*. Raymond's parents, Marie and Frank, live in the lifestyle of nostalgia that I'm referring to. In particular, the scenes from their house; the wallpaper, furniture, and dated gender roles makes us utter the phrase, "Remember when…." Another example is shown in the sitcom *Frasier*. Marty Crane, appearing to be in his 70's, has an iconic, yet dated, lounge chair in the upscale Seattle apartment belonging to his son, Frasier, that is often the topic of debate. Marty insists on keeping his favorite chair even though it is a complete misfit amongst the other lavish décor. I can relate to this plot when I notice furniture and décor from my childhood still proudly displayed at my parents' house.

Another fine depiction of elders dated life-style is shown in the *Progressive Insurance* Commercials where Dr. Rick, Parenta-Life Coach, helps people to avoid behaving like their parents. Printing airline tickets, never clearing out the freezer, asking for discounts at stores, being shocked at movie theater snack prices, and leaving events early to avoid parking lot traffic are just some of the behaviors Dr. Rick addresses. I laugh out loud every time these commercials come on because they are so spot on!

The elderly tend to hang on to styles and items from their past. Many older women seem especially partial to hairstyles they sported some 30 years ago. The older men seem attached to their wardrobe, especially old sports and concert T-shirts. People grow attached to styles and items that brought them joy or remind them of a loved one or happy time. The elderly may also hold on to items with the philosophy in mind that if it isn't broke, no need to replace. My family refers to this inclination as the Depression Era Mindset, which is a diminishing one. We currently live in a spend happy time where buying items is just a computer click away and quite cost efficient. (It's no wonder none of us can figure out what gifts to buy anybody). Many elderlies live on a fixed income and do not have the means to stay updated with the trends. Additionally, the elderly, as previously mentioned, have gained new perspective on life and the material items and competitiveness of following the trends is simply not as important as it used to be.

Now that I have suggested that elderly people are stuck in a time warp, I must also acknowledge the contradicting reality that they are the generation forced to adapt to several significant changes. Simply put, the longer you live, the more changes are forced upon you. Older generations are forced to adapt to: retirement, reduced income, diminishing health, decreased productivity, increased death of loved ones, role transformations, technology developments, changing political and social views, increasing environmental issues, and all of the physical and emotional changes to themselves that come with aging. So, when we think of our elderly parents as time capsules, we must remember all the changes over many years they've been brave enough to endure.

Stick to the Routine

Another common and rather odd behavior of the elderly is their inability to do more than one single activity on any given day. Even if they still maintain the energy level and physicality, many elderlies will only allow themselves to partake in one event per day. In my own experience, both parents and grandparents are delighted to have company, but only for a short period of time. I suspect, that visiting too long will interrupt their daily routine which they find so comforting. Many elderlies are weary of leaving their house, especially if spontaneously suggested. I have noticed that if not planned weeks in advance and clearly written in pen on the calendar, an invitation to take them to lunch will certainly be accompanied by the excuse that it is laundry day and therefore, no can do. Or, perhaps, their 3:00 dentist appointment will keep them planted for the day, or week.

At the Assisted Living Center, I will prompt the residents that it is time to make their way down to chair exercise class. I'm immediately told by many that they are unable to attend class because they already had or will have an event that day. Some will tell me that they have Bingo at 3:00. When I explain to them that exercise begins at One O'clock and only lasts 40 minutes, I get the look of curse. Two activities in a day is just too much. On Sundays, most will not come to class if they have already attended a church service that morning. If they are having a visitor on exercise day, no way in hell will they be able to make it, even if their visitor has come and gone. Many stay planted in anticipation of a phone call. My favorite alibi is when I'm told that they can't attend class because they haven't had their daily bowel movement.

I've always wondered why older people stick so closely to their daily routine and why interruptions make them nutty. I've also struggled to understand why they are so reluctant to maintain a semi-busy schedule. But the older I get, the more I empathize and even relate to this phenomenon.

First, adhering to a schedule is predictable and safe. It is human nature, at any age, to feel more at ease with a predictable routine. As we age, we come to appreciate comfort more than excitement. Sticking to the daily routine helps to alleviate the necessity of making adjustments that could ultimately have a snowball effect of uncomfortable repercussions. For example, my father knows how much physical energy he can exert in any given day before he pays the physical price in the following days. If I invite him to the Botanical Gardens, he will need to adjust his physical exertion in advance to reserve for that day. Otherwise, joint pain flares, resulting in poor sleep, headaches, crabbiness, and irregular bowel movements.

Second, wanting to keep life simple may have a lot to do with the idea that the elderly "have already been there… done that." Our most industrious years obviously take place when we are younger, attempting to fulfill so many responsibilities and curiosities. The desire to travel, attend concerts, go to restaurants, wander through stores, etc. is not as appealing when done for so many years. Think about this: we all have an appetite for a little Rest and Relaxation and therefore we take vacations to escape the rat race. Vacations are a means to temporarily rid our lives from "having" to do anything." Once retired, the R and R craving remains and retirement affords one the opportunity to be on permanent vacation where time is less relevant.

Third, research suggests that the elderly may find it difficult to adjust their routines and habits because of the deterioration of a brain circuit that affects their ability to select the most appropriate action in response to unfamiliar or changing environments. In other words, the elderly brains are less capable of flexibility. When an older person finds themselves in a new circumstance, they will become more confused and frustrated than younger generations where the brain has the ability to quickly adjust (Science Daily, 2014 & Ians, 2016). I notice this phenomenon in the residents I work with. If their schedule changes for any reason, it tends to send them into a bit of a tailspin. It takes time for their minds to sort through the change so they know how to proceed with their day.

Fourth, the elderly stick to routines and an uncomplicated lifestyle because, quite simply, they are tired! Bodies are worn out, minds have stilled, and the thrill of activity has faded.

Flatulence

My Grandma Adele, deceased many moons ago, would stand from her chair and, without fail, a loud burst of air would ruffle her butt cheeks. And every fart was followed by a declaration, "I'm celebrating!" I find my friends at the Assisted Living Center also celebrating from their asses on a daily basis. The odd smell in old people's homes, I declare, is due to persistent and stale farts.

If you haven't noticed, the older you get, the more you fart. Now this is kind of fun. We have laughed at farts our entire life, for in most cultures, ripping one is somehow funny. The emission of air out of any other orifice, like burps or queefs (vaginal air), is just not as laughable. But for some reason, butt gas is hilarious for audiences and usually embarrassing for the blower. So why do older people fart more than the young?

As we age, our digestive system becomes more sensitive to the food we put into our bodies. For example, it is quite common for the elderly to be lactose and/or fructose intolerant. When food is difficult to digest, the result will often be expulsion of gas. Further, constipation is a common symptom of the aging GI tract and therefore, the elderly are encouraged to eat foods that are high in fiber. Yet, foods that are high in fiber also result in gassiness. Medications can also be a cause for increased gas. Some medications simply have flatulence as a side effect and other medications may not be digestion friendly. So, whether you think it is fun or not, the slowing digestive tract in aging individuals can be cause for flatulence celebration!

My daughters tell me that I, too, have become a frequent farter. I tried to blame the high elevation. But the reality is, with age comes an increase in flatulence! I've given up on trying to hold a fart in or sneak it out without being identified. Both remedies are a bad idea. So like my late Grandma Adele, my ass and I will proudly celebrate growing old!

- -

Changing behavior in seniors, although it can seem funny and strange, can also be an indicator of more serious problems. If the behavior seems to diminish their ability to care for themselves or if they seem to rapidly regress, it is time to see a physician. Some behaviors that may be of greater concern include, aggression, poor hygiene, inappropriate language in public, paranoia, hording, extreme money mismanagement, and constantly demanding of attention. These behaviors may be signs of Dementia or other illnesses.

Summary

There is no doubt that aging people often display peculiar behavior. Our society pokes fun of this all the time. But if we really think about it, all of the aforementioned odd behavior is actually quite natural and expected considering what we know about the aging process. Realizing that there are logical reasons for repetitious stories, dated styles, daily simplicity, and fart frenzies can help us to be more patient and understanding with our aging loved ones.

Chapter 14

Resolve

I've shared my story; my trepidation of growing old. My view of aging, once quite negative and discouraging, has evolved into a more hopeful reckoning.

My 30-plus years as a teacher allotted me the privilege to stay connected with young minds, bodies, and souls. It kept me in a world where only *I* aged and my students, rotating in and out of my life, were forever young. I found youthfulness to be so intoxicating. As it slowly disappeared from me, I gripped tighter; not willing to accept my aging self.

Out of desperation, I joined millions of other women in an attempt to fool the world into thinking that I was still young. I fought the changes to my body with products and methods and adopted the ideology that I could somehow stall time. It was important to me that I remained likeable which required that I fit into the prescribed mold for attractiveness and desirability.

I grossly underestimated the changes I would endure as a result of motherhood as well as hormone variations. I did not expect to feel insignificant as my roles changed, nor did I ever anticipate having to make so many adaptions for my changing body and mind. I never thought I would find myself scrambling for purpose. The inability to control these unexpected developments made me feel helpless and lost.

I was never prepared for being negatively judged simply due to my rise in years. Until now, ageism was an irrelevant concept for me.

I low lucky I was to have planted my tormented self into the forgiving mountains where I am reminded of the natural rhythm of life. Separated from my familiar audience, I was finally given the opportunity to free myself from expectations. Whether by coincidence or destiny, a new and much older audience came into my life to demonstrate and teach me how to love my aging self. I'm convinced that this gift was not meant solely for me. I am teacher and therefore, I share this enlightenment with others.

At the trailhead, we must acknowledge the many challenges that women can expect as they hike the aging course. We have to admit that there is no fountain of youth and that the constant chase for it can be unsatisfying and quite expensive. The products and procedures we seek to reduce our age are just a temporary delay to the summit. Further, we mustn't view our aging self so negatively, for that is a misrepresentation of our true warrior-like strength.

As we begin the climb, may we be reminded that the trail will be both difficult and exhilarating. Changing bodies, roles, and identities will take courage and grit. We cannot allow others to define for us what it means to be beautiful and old. Instead, we must promote our own definitions and assist our trail-mates in validating our aging selves.

There will be times during our hike that we will feel threatened or scared by the unfamiliar surroundings. Don't be deterred by those forces attempting to make your journey more complicated. Stay strong. Be courageous.

Pack lightly, for the journey is long. When we reach into our backpacks for the tools we need, let there be the right nourishment to feed our souls. We must come equipped with the ability to recognize the ageist boulders that will attempt to block our trail. Being equipped with *optimism* will prove to be the most helpful tool on your hike.

We should be prepared for stumbles. Sometimes our bodies will slow us down and our minds may lose its direction. We have to adapt to the changes and not get lost. Stay the course and continue engaging in the activities you enjoy with the people you love.

The hike must not be taken alone. Always know that there are trail-mates who may be experiencing similar obstacles. Talk about it. Share your fears as well as your wisdom. Perhaps other hikers can assist you with the climb; let them, for the top should not feel lonely.

Don't worry about your pace on the hike. You will arrive at the summit when you are supposed to. But until then, appreciate the present. Fancy yourself with being fully invested in the moment. Your trail will need your full attention so that you don't miss the color and wonderment it will undoubtedly offer.

Take the time, on your hike, to allow the landscape around you – the touch of nature – to seep into your bones. Nature will be the one entity powerful enough to tame the ego and ignite your spirit. Remember not to take your hike so seriously. Find the moments to behave oddly; perhaps mimic the birds and make others' laugh. Laugh at yourself.

As you near the mountain top, exhale. It is the perfect time for gratitude. It is here that you will finally appreciate the view. You will appear so small amongst the vastness of the mountain range, trees, valley, and sky. You will most likely feel proud of your conquest and eager to let the world know that you made it! And as much as you wish to hold onto this sight forever, the light of the moon will remind you that it is time to descend. Do so with the satisfaction of knowing that others will follow in your path and will be grateful for your example.

Chapter 15

Miles to Go

So here I am, in a quiet place with new room to breathe. As amazing as it feels to be free from so many former obligations, I know that I have yet to complete my life's hike. I thrive on the thought of knowing that I still have something to offer this world and that it will be received with the kind of gratitude that I feel towards this awakening. I am ready to stop chasing the past. I am ready to shed the fear I have about growing old. Nature will run its course whether I like it or not. The river will continue to run, the birds to sing, the geese to fly.

I know that I am not alone in thought. The idea of an Aging Enlightenment; an emergence of a healthy definition of aging beautifully, was born out of the recognition that all women hike the same paths and could use a trail-mate. We need to engage ourselves in honest conversations about our struggle with aging. Every story has a lesson. Every woman has a triumph.

For all the daughters, sisters, and friends who are just at the trail head; I hope your hike comes with a better map than I initially had. Know that aging is tough. Understand that the natural changes to your body and mind don't need to be reversed or feel crippling. Each phase of the process is an opportunity to re-invent a more sophisticated you. Stay vigilant in keeping that glorious vessel healthy. Educate yourself on the practices that will give you the peace of mind to mature as you are meant to. Growing old doesn't have to feel burdensome; simply give yourself permission to do it.

I am 51 years old. My summit is miles away and I am not ready to descend. How I get there will be simple, one step at a time.

Bibliography

Alter, A. (2017). *Irresistible: The Rise of Addictive Technology and the Business of Keeping Us Hooked.* Penguin Press.

Americans Spent Over $8.7 Billion on Aesthetic Plastic Surgery in the First 6 Months of 2021. (2021). *The Aesthetic Society.* https://www.theaestheticsociety.org

Arias, E., Tejada-Vera B., & Ahmad F. (2020). Vital Statistics Rapid Release. *U.S. Department of Health & Human Services, Centers for Disease Control.* www.cdc.gov/nchs/data/vsrr/VSRR10-508.pdf

Assisted Living (2022). *Health in Aging.* https://healthinaging.org/age-friendly-healthcare-you/care-settings/assisted-living

The Average Cost of Senior Living: Can You Afford It? (2022). *SeniorLiving.org.* https://assistedliving.org/senior-housing/the-average-cost-of-senior-living

Berger, S. (2018, June). Tech-free Dinners and No Smartphones Past 10 pm- How Steve Jobs, Bill Gates and Mark Cuban Limited Their Kids Screen Time. *CNBC, Make It.* https://cnbc.com/2018/06/05/how-bil-gates-mark-cuban-and-others-limit-their-kids-tech-use.html

Bradley-Bursack, C. (2022). What to Do When a Senior Repeats the Same Things Over and Over. *Aging Care.* https://www.agingcare.com/articles/elders-repeating-the-same-story

Brown University (2014). Many Older Brains Have Plasticity, but in a Different Place. *Science Daily.* www.sciencedaily.com/releases/2014/11/141119084947htm

Castellano, D. (2021). Botox Statistics You Need to Know in 2021. *Elite Plastic Surgery.* https://www.elitetampa.com

Chang, E. (2019). Taking the Mystery out of Botox and Dermal Fillers. *American Society of Plastic Surgeons.* https://www.plasticsurgery.org/news/blog/taking-the-mystery-out-of-botox-and-dermal-fillers

Cherry, K. (2021). Erik Erikson's Stages of Psychosocial Development. *VeryWellMind.* www.verywellmind.com/erik-eriksons-stages-of-psychosocial-development

Celebre, A. & Waggoner Denton, A. (2014). The Good, the Bad, and the Ugly of the Dove Campaign for Real Beauty. *The Inquisitive Mind.* (Issue 19). https://www.in-mind.org/article/the-good-the-bad-and-the-ugly-of-the-dove-campaign-for-real-beauty

Ciotti, S. (2020). *Breezing Through Menopause: A Holistic Doctor's Customized Approach to Hormonal Change.*

Cohut, M. (2020). The Controversy of 'Female Hysteria.' *Medical News Today.* https://www.mecicalnewstoday.com/articles/the-controversy-of-female-hysteria

Cosmetic Surgery Market. (2022). *GlobeNewswire.* www.globenewswire.com

Dementia. (2021). *Mayo Clinic.* https://www.mayoclinic.org/diseases-conditions/dementia/symptoms-causes/syc

Dimovski, A. (2020, March). 20 Eye-Opening Statistics About the State of Career Changes in 2022. *GoRemotely.* www.goremotely.net/blog/career-change-statistics/

Does Ageism Exist in All Cultures? (2022). *Every Age Counts.* www.everyagecounts.org.au/does-ageism-exist-in-all-cultures

Get the Facts on Economic Security for Seniors. (2021, March). *National Council on Aging.* www.ncoa.org/article/get-the-facts-on-economic-security-for-seniors

Gibson, William E. (2019, March). Nearly Half of Americans 55+ Have No Retirement Savings. *AARP.* https://www.aarp.org/retirement/retirement-savings/info-2019/no-retirement-money-saved.html

Faludi, S. (1991). *Backlash: The Undeclared War Against American Women.* Anchor Books, Doubleday.

Gannon, M. (2012, Dec). Optimism is Key to Successful Aging. *LiveScience.* www.livescience.com/25327-optimism-sucessful-aging.html

Heerema, E. (2020). The Problems with Elderspeak. *Verywell Health.* https://www.verywellhealth.com/elder speak-and-older-adults-97972

How to Handle Your Elderly Parent's Unusual Behavior. (2018). *C-Care.* https://www.c-care.ca/blog.dementia/handle-elderly-parents-unusual-behaviour/

Howard, B. (2019, July). Sleep Medication Linked to Dementia. *AARP.* https://aarp/health/dementia/info-2019/dementia-sleep-medication.html

Hoyt, J. (2022, June). How Much Does Assisted Living and Home Care Cost in the U.S.? *SeniorLiving.Org.* www.seniorliving.org/assisted-living/costs/

Harvey A. Friedman Center for Aging (2021, Sept). Ageism-The Unnoticed-ism. *Washington University in St. Louis, Institute for Public Health.* www.publichealth. wustl.edu/ageism-the-unnoticed-ism/

Ians, S. (2016, April). Here's Why Older People Find It Tough to Adjust to new Surroundings. *Hindustan Times.* www.hindustantimes.com/health-and-fitness/here-s-why-older-people-find-it-toudh-to-adjust-to-new-surroundings/story-t5jd1rWbFAkfkCLZBI16iN.html

Jobs with Mandatory Retirement. (2022). *Career Trend.* www.careertrend.com/jobs-mandatory-retirement-7991.html

Kaslow, K. (2021,May). Ageism in American Culture. *Keystone Elder Law P.C.* www.keystoneelderlaw.com/ageism-in-american-culture/

Kita, J. (2019, Dec). Workplace Age Discrimination in America: It's Time to Step Up and Stop the Last Acceptable Bias. *AARP.* www.aarp/work/age-discrimination/still-thrives-in-america/

Lafee, S. (2018). Stats Show Cosmetic Surgery Numbers are Plastic. *UC San Diego Health.* https://health. ucsd.edu/news/features/Pages/2019-01-07-listicle-Stats-Show-Cosmetic-Surgery-Numbers-are-Plastic.aspx

Levitin, D. (2020). *Successful Aging: A Neuroscientist Explores the Power and Potential of Our Lives.* Dutton, Penguin Random House.

Mejia, Z. (2018, Jan). Apple CEO Tim Cook: Don't Let Your Kids Use Social Media. *CNBC, Make It.* https://cnbc. com/2018/01/23/apple-ceo-tim-cook-dont-let-your-kids-use-social-media.html

Melore, C. (2022). Be Positive, Stay Young: The Secret to Healthy Aging May be Optimism. *StudyFinds.* www.studyfinds.org/healthy-aging-and-optimism/

Morrison, S. (2021). Defying Ageism. *The Millie Report.* (pp 14-19).

Oliver, D. (2021, April). Ageism Still Lurks in Hollywood, according to analysis of female film characters. *USA Today.* https://usatoday.com/story/entertainment/movies/2021/04/13

O'Malley, S. (2016). *Advice from my 80-Year-Old Self: Real Words of Wisdom from People Ages 7 to 88.* Chronical Books.

Optimism and Healthy Aging in Women. (2019). *National Library of Medicine.* www.ncbi.nih.gov

Paddock, C. (2015, July). Over-the-Counter Sleep Aids Linked to Dementia. *Medical News Today.* https://medicalnewstoday.com/articles/288546#

Pipher, M. (2019). *Women Rowing North: Navigating Life's Currents and Flourishing As We Age.* Bloomsbury Publishing.

Plastic Surgery Statistics (2020). *American Society of Plastic Surgeons,* Connect. www.plasticsurgery.org/new/plastic-surgery-statistics

Puig, A. (2011). *Reinventing Yourself: Overcome Your Anxiety and Fear when Faced with Life's Problems and Challenges.* MJF Books.

Rajan, V. (2022). Why Seniors Pass Gas and What You Can Do About It. *Aging Care.* https://www.agingcare.com/topics/147/senior-health

Rehm, D. (2016). *On My Own.* Alfred A. Knopf.

Salam, M. (2018). *For Online Daters, Women Peak at 18 While Men Peak at 50, Study Finds. OY.* The New York Times. https://www.nytimes.com/2018/08/15/style/dating-apps-online-men-women-age.html

Sarmiento, S. (2021). The Lingering Effects of Female Hysteria in Medicine. *Berkeley Political Review.* https://bpr.berkeley.edu/2021/08/10/the-lingering-effects-of-female-hysteria-in-medicine/

The Science of Living Longer (2019, Nov). *Special Time Magazine Edition.*

Sollitto, M. (2021). How to Deal with Aging Parents' Difficult Behaviors. *Aging Care.* https://www.agingcare.com/articles

Ten Early Signs and Symptoms of Alzheimer's. (2022). *Alzheimer's Association.* https://www.alz.org/alzheimers-dementia/10_signs

Townley, C. (2019). Cosmetic Surgery is on the Rise, New Data Reveal. *Medical News Today.* https://www.medicalnewstoday.com/articles/324693

Twenge, J. (2017*). iGen: Why Today's Super-Connected Kids Are Growing Up Less Rebellious, More Tolerant, Less Happy- and Completely Unprepared for Adulthood.* Atria Books.

U.S. Burden of Alzheimer's Disease, Related Dementias to double by 2060. (2018, Sept). *Centers for Disease Control and Prevention.* www.cdc.gov/media/releases/2018/p0920-alzheimers-burden-double-2060.html

Villines, Z. (2021, Nov). What Is Ageism, and How Does It Affect Health? *Medical News Today.* www. medicalnewstoday.com/articles/ageism

Viorst, J. (2002). *Necessary Losses: The Loves, Illusions, Dependencies, and Impossible Expectations that All of Us have to Give Up In Order to Grow.* The Free Press.

Wade, L. (2015, July). OK Cupid Data on Sex, Desirability, and Age. *The Society Pages*, Sociological. www.thesocietypages.org/socimages/2015/07/03/0k-cupid-data-on-sex-desirability-and-age/

Wilson, C.(2015, Oct). This Chart Shows Hollywood's Glaring Gender Gap. *Time.* https://time.com/4062700/hollywood-gender-gap/

Woodruff, J. (2021, Dec). Older Americans Make Up Majority of Covid Deaths. They are Falling Behind on Boosters. *PBS.* www.pbs.org/newshour/show/older-americans-make-up-a-majority-of-covid-deaths-they-are-falling-behind-on-boosters

17 Remarkable Career Change Statistics to Know, (2022, March). *Apollo Technical.* https://www.apollotechnical.com/career-chang-statistics

Acknowledgments

Thank you, Josh, my greatest love, for editing, listening, and supporting. Growing old with YOU is the best part of the hike.

Thank you, my maturing friends, for sharing, laughing, and inspiring me to push this aging dialogue. What amazing trail-mates I have.

Thank you, dear moms and dads for cheering me on. I love that you think I am capable.

Thank you, Ryan, for the beautiful logo

and for your creative assistance.

Thank you, Fyra▲ for the fabulous cover design.

Thank you, Brian Banash for the awesome Rocky Mountain graphic.

Thank you, Dane for the music compositions for the audio. Your talent moves me.

Thank you, Doug at Eagle Sound for your dedication to recording the audio.

Connect with Me:
Glassmoonretreats@gmail.com

*If you found this book helpful
and/or entertaining,
please leave a review on Amazon.com*